MAUS

PANTHEON B

AUS

A SURVIVOR'S TALE

I

MY FATHER BLEEDS HISTORY

art spiegelman

KS NEW YORK

"The Jews are undoubtedly a race,
but they are not human."
Adolf Hitler

Thanks to Ken and Flo Jacobs, Ernie Gehr, Paul Pavel, Louise Fili, and Steven Heller,
whose appreciation and moral support have helped this book find its shape.

Thanks to Mala Spiegelman for her help in translating Polish books and documents,
and for wanting *Maus* to happen.

And thanks to Françoise Mouly for her intelligence and integrity,
for her editorial skills, and for her love.

Chapters 1 through 6 first appeared, in somewhat different form, in *Raw* magazine between 1980 and 1985.

"Prisoner on the Hell Planet" originally appeared in *Short Order Comix #1*, 1973

Library of Congress Cataloging-in-Publication Data
Spiegelman, Art.
Maus: a survivor's tale.
I: My Father Bleeds History
1. Spiegelman, Vladek — Comic books, strips, etc.
2. Holocaust, Jewish (1939-1945) — Poland — Biography Comic books, strips, etc.
3. Holocaust survivors — United States — Biography — Comic books, strips, etc.
4. Spiegelman, Art — Comic books, strips, etc.
5. Children of the Holocaust survivors — United States — Biography — Comic books, strips, etc.
I. Title.
D810.J4S643   1986   940.53'15'03924024   86-42642
ISBN 0-394-74723-2

For more information about *Raw* magazine, write to Raw Books and Graphics,
27 Greene Street, New York, New York 10013.

Manufactured in U.S.A.

85 84 83 82

Rego Park, N.Y. c.1958

5

MY FATHER BLEEDS HISTORY

(MID-1930s TO WINTER 1944)

ONTENTS

FOR ANJA

I went out to see my Father in Rego Park. I hadn't seen him in a long time- we weren't that close.

POPPA!

OI, ARTIE. YOU'RE LATE. I WAS WORRIED.

IT'S A SHAME FRANÇOISE ALSO DIDN'T COME.

UH-HUH. SHE SENDS REGARDS.

He had aged a lot since I saw him last. My Mother's suicide and his two heart attacks had taken their toll.

MALA! LOOK WHO'S HERE! **ARTIE!**

He was remarried. Mala knew my parents in Poland before the war.

She was a survivor too, like most of my parents' friends.

HI, ARTIE. LET ME TAKE YOUR COAT.

THE DINNER IS ON THE TABLE.

ACCH, MALA!

A **WIRE** HANGER YOU GIVE HIM! I HAVEN'T SEEN ARTIE IN ALMOST TWO YEARS- WE HAVE PLENTY **WOODEN** HANGERS.

They didn't get along.

After dinner he took me into my old room...

COME- WE'LL TALK WHILE I PEDAL...

IT'S GOOD FOR MY HEART, THE PEDALING. BUT, TELL ME, HOW IS IT BY YOU? HOW IS GOING THE COMICS BUSINESS?

I STILL WANT TO DRAW THAT BOOK ABOUT YOU...

THE ONE I USED TO TALK TO YOU ABOUT...

ABOUT YOUR LIFE IN POLAND, AND THE WAR.

IT WOULD TAKE **MANY** BOOKS, MY LIFE, AND NO ONE WANTS ANYWAY TO HEAR SUCH STORIES.

I WANT TO HEAR IT. START WITH MOM... TELL ME HOW YOU MET.

BETTER YOU SHOULD SPEND YOUR TIME TO MAKE DRAWINGS WHAT WILL BRING YOU SOME MONEY...

BUT, IF YOU WANT, I CAN TELL YOU...I LIVED THEN IN CZESTOCHOWA, A SMALL CITY NOT FAR FROM THE BOR-DER OF GERMANY...

I WAS IN TEXTILES- BUY-ING AND SELLING- I DIDNT MAKE MUCH, BUT ALWAYS I COULD MAKE A *LIVING*.

12

I WAS, AT THAT TIME, YOUNG, AND REALLY A NICE, HANDSOME BOY.

I HAD A LOT OF GIRLS WHAT I DIDN'T EVEN *KNOW* THAT WOULD RUN AFTER ME.

RRING

HELLO, VLADEK? THIS IS YULEK...

A FRIEND OF MINE, LUCIA GREENBERG, WOULD LIKE TO BE INTRODUCED TO YOU.

THE SHEIK

PEOPLE ALWAYS TOLD ME I LOOKED JUST LIKE RUDOLPH VALENTINO.

PICTURE

EVENTUALLY, I TOOK LUCIA TO DANCE...

DO YOU LIVE ALONE?

YES.

I HAVE A SMALL APARTMENT. MY PARENTS MOVED TO SOSNOWIEC.

I'D LIKE TO SEE IT SOMETIME.

MAYBE SOMETIME.

WHEREVER I WENT - I LOOKED AROUND - AND LUCIA GREENBERG WOULD BE ALSO THERE...

VLADEK!- WHICH WAY ARE YOU GOING?

JUST TO THE MARKET.

ME TOO - LET'S WALK TOGETHER.

BUT, POP,... MOM'S NAME WAS ANNA ZYLBERBERG!...

ALL THIS WAS *BEFORE* I MET ANJA - JUST LISTEN, YES?

WHY DON'T YOU EVER INVITE ME TO YOUR HOME?... ARE YOU ASHAMED OF IT?

SHE KEPT INSISTING ME TO SHOW HER MY APARTMENT...

-SO FINALLY, I INVITED HER...

EVERYTHING'S SO NEAT AND CLEAN!

I LIKE TO KEEP THINGS IN ORDER.

YOU MUST HAVE ANOTHER GIRL-FRIEND WHO CLEANS FOR YOU-NO?

NO.

...I DIDN'T WANT TO BE MORE CLOSER WITH HER, BUT SHE REALLY WOULDN'T LET ME GO.

14

15

THE NEXT MORNING WE ALL MET TOGETHER. MY COUSIN AND ANJA SPOKE SOMETIMES IN ENGLISH.

HOW YOU LIKE HIM?

HE'S A HANDSOME BOY AND SEEMS VERY NICE.

THEY COULDN'T KNOW I UNDERSTOOD.

WELL- I PROMISED TO BE HOME EARLY... I'LL LEAVE YOU TWO ALONE

YOU KNOW, YOU SHOULD BE CAREFUL SPEAKING ENGLISH- A "STRANGER" COULD UNDERSTAND.

Y-YOU KNOW ENGLISH?

DID YOU STUDY IT IN SCHOOL?

I HAD TO QUIT SCHOOL AT ABOUT 14 TO WORK.

...BUT I TOOK PRIVATE LESSONS... I ALWAYS DREAMED OF GOING TO AMERICA.

IT'S A SHAME YOU HAVE TO RETURN TO CZESTOCHOWA SO SOON.

YES- BUT I HAVE MY BUSINESS.

HAVE YOU A PHONE AT HOME?

AS SOON I CAME BACK TO CZESTOCHOWA, SHE CALLED - ONCE A DAY... TWICE... EVERY DAY WE TALKED.

AND THEN SHE STARTED WRITING TO ME SUCH BEAUTIFUL LETTERS— ALMOST NOBODY COULD WRITE POLISH LIKE SHE WROTE.

I VISITED A COUPLE TIMES TO HER. SHE SENT ME A PHOTO...

I BOUGHT A VERY NICE FRAME...

IT PASSED MAYBE A WEEK UNTIL LUCIA AGAIN CAME AND SAW THE PHOTO...

I'M GOING TO GET EN- GAGED TO HER, LUCIA.

PSSH! AND LOOK AT WHAT A **BEAUTY** YOU PICKED.

LOOKS AREN'T EVERYTHING, LUCIA. IT ISN'T GOOD FOR EITHER OF US THAT YOU KEEP COMING UP HERE...

"...WE HAVE TO PLAN FOR OUR FUTURES, AND—

FORGET HER! LET ME MAKE YOU HAPPY!

IT WAS NOT SO EASY TO GET FREE FROM LUCIA.

17

MOM WASN'T THAT ATTRACTIVE, HUH?

NOT SO LIKE LUCIA,... BUT IF YOU TALKED A LITTLE TO HER, YOU STARTED LOVING HER MORE AND MORE.

ONE TIME WE WALKED INTO THE DIRECTOR FROM HER SCHOOL.

YOU'RE VERY LUCKY, MR. SPIEGELMAN.

...YOU DON'T KNOW WHAT A GIRL YOU'RE GETTING—I'VE HAD MANY STUDENTS...

...BUT NEVER ONE AS SENSITIVE AND INTELLIGENT AS ANNA!

YES—THAT'S WHY I PICKED HER.

I WISH YOU COULD VISIT ME IN CZESTOCHOWA—I'D LIKE TO SHOW YOU OFF TO MY FRIENDS.

I'VE BEGGED MY MOTHER TO LET ME GO—BUT SHE'S SO RELIGIOUS AND OLD-FASHIONED.

...SHE WOULD NEVER ALLOW ME TO GO TO A BACHELOR'S APARTMENT!

ANJA'S PARENTS WERE ANXIOUS SHE SHOULD BE MARRIED. SHE WAS 24; I WAS THEN 30.

OH, MY PARENTS WOULD LIKE YOU TO COME TO DINNER TOMORROW NIGHT.

THE ZYLBERBERG FAMILY WAS VERY WELL OFF—MILLIONAIRES!

18

THE ZYLBERBERGS HAD A HOSIERY FACTORY—ONE OF THE BIGGEST IN POLAND... BUT WHEN I CAME IN TO THEIR HOUSE IT WAS SO LIKE A KING CAME...

WELCOME, WELCOME.

ANJA — VLADEK IS HERE!

MAKE YOURSELF COMFORTABLE WHILE I HELP WITH THE DINNER.

TO SEE WHAT A HOUSEKEEPER SHE WAS, I PEEKED INTO ANJA'S CLOSET.

EVERYTHING IS NEAT AND STRAIGHT JUST THE WAY I LIKE IT!

BUT WHAT'S THIS — PILLS?!

I WROTE DOWN EVERY PILL.

IF SHE WAS SICK, THEN WHAT DID I NEED IT FOR?

DINNER IS READY!

LATER, A FRIEND, A DRUGGIST, TOLD ME THE PILLS WERE ONLY BECAUSE SHE WAS SO SKINNY AND NERVOUS.

HOW ABOUT SOME MORE GEFILTE FISH, VLADEK?

SO, TO MAKE A LONG STORY SHORT, BY THE END OF 1936 WE WERE ENGAGED AND I MOVED FROM CZESTOCHOWA TO SOSNOWIEC.

ACH! HERE I FORGOT TO TELL SOMETHING FROM *BEFORE* I MOVED TO SOSNOWIEC BUT AFTER OUR ENGAGEMENT WAS MADE.

ONE EVENING THE BELL RANG ...

LUCIA

WHAT ARE YOU DOING HERE? I'M ON MY WAY OUT.

I-I'LL COME WITH YOU.

NO, YOU CAN'T COME WI-

PLEASE, VLADEK!

SHE FELL ON THE FLOOR AND HELD STRONG MY LEGS.

DON'T RUN AWAY!

I SAW NOW THAT I WENT TOO FAR WITH HER.

SLAM!

I RAN OUT TO MY FRIEND WHAT INTRO-DUCED US. HE WENT TO CALM HER DOWN AND TOOK HER HOME.

I DIDN'T HEAR MORE FROM LUCIA - BUT ALSO I STOPPED HEARING FROM ANJA ...

NO TELEPHONE CALLS, NO LETTERS, *NOTHING!* WHAT HAPPENED?

HELLO, MRS. ZYLBERBERG. COULD I SPEAK TO ANJA?

SHE SAYS SHE WON'T SPEAK TO YOU!

BUT *WHY?*

SHE GOT A LETTER FROM SOMEONE IN CZESTOCHOWA. MY GOD! IT SAYS THE WORST THINGS IN THE WORLD ABOUT YOU!

WELL, I CAN'T CONVINCE HER ON THE PHONE. I'LL COME DOWN BY TRAIN ON FRIDAY AFTER WORK.

IT WASN'T EVEN A HOLIDAY, BUT I WENT ANYWAY TO SOSNOWIEC.

SO, TELL ME, ANJA - WHAT HAVE I DONE THAT'S SO HORRIBLE?

YOU SHOULD KNOW- JUST READ *THIS!*

21

BUT THIS WHAT I JUST TOLD YOU—ABOUT LUCIA AND SO— I DON'T WANT YOU SHOULD WRITE THIS IN YOUR BOOK.

WHAT? WHY NOT?

IT HAS NOTHING TO DO WITH HITLER, WITH THE HOLOCAUST!

BUT POP— IT'S GREAT MATERIAL. IT MAKES EVERYTHING MORE REAL— MORE HUMAN.

I WANT TO TELL YOUR STORY, THE WAY IT REALLY HAPPENED.

BUT THIS ISN'T SO PROPER, SO RESPECTFUL.

... I CAN TELL YOU OTHER STORIES, BUT SUCH PRIVATE THINGS, I DON'T WANT YOU SHOULD MENTION.

OKAY, OKAY— I PROMISE.

For the next few months I went back to visit my father quite regularly, to hear his story.

EVEN AFTER THE MARRIAGE, WHEN THIS FELLOW CAME TO SOSNOWIEC, ANJA ALWAYS RAN TO SEE HIM.

I DIDN'T KNOW, OF COURSE, THAT HE WAS COMMUNIST. I **ALWAYS** KEPT FAR AWAY FROM COMMUNIST PEOPLE.

A LITTLE AFTER WE WERE MARRIED I CAME HOME FROM A SELLING TRIP...

POLICIA

HEY VLADEK—THEY JUST ARRESTED THE SEAMSTRESS THAT LIVES DOWN YOUR HALL!...

SHE HAD SOME SECRET COMMUNIST DOCUMENTS!

AND WHEN I WENT UPSTAIRS...

THE POLICE JUST ARRES—HUH? WHAT'S THE MATTER?

THE POLICE WERE **HERE!**

LOOKING FOR ANJA!

SHE JUST TOLD US...

THAT BOY FROM WARSAW BRINGS COMMUNIST MESSAGES.

SHE TRANSLATES THEM INTO GERMAN AND PASSES THEM ON!

ANJA WAS INVOLVED IN *CONSPIRATIONS!*

WHEN I FOUND OUT THIS STORY, I WAS READY TO BREAK THE MARRIAGE.

I TOLD HER "ANJA, IF YOU WANT ME YOU HAVE TO GO MY WAY...

IF YOU WANT YOUR COMMUNIST FRIENDS, THEN I CAN'T STAY IN THIS HOUSE!"

AND SHE WAS A GOOD GIRL, AND OF COURSE SHE STOPPED ALL SUCH THINGS.

WHAT HAPPENED TO THE SEAMSTRESS?

MISS STEFANSKA SAT IN PRISON FOR A LONGER TIME — MAYBE 3 MONTHS.

IT WASN'T ENOUGH EVIDENCE AND FINALLY THE POLICE LEFT HER GO.

FATHER-IN-LAW PAID THE COST FROM THE LAWYERS AND GAVE TO HER SOME MONEY—IT COST MAYBE 15,000 ZLOTYS.

THAT'S A LOT, HUH?

JA, BUT NOT ONLY THIS. AT THE SAME TIME HE DID FOR US EVEN *MORE*...

YOU KNOW, VLADEK, WHEN YOU AND ANJA GIVE ME A GRANDCHILD, I WANT HIM TO BE WELL-OFF.

WELL, I ALMOST HAVE ENOUGH FROM MY SALES TRIPS TO START UP A TEXTILE SHOP...

A SHOP? PFUI! YOU OUGHT TO HAVE A TEXTILE *FACTORY!*

THAT WOULD COST A *FORTUNE!!*

PLEASE— I CAN GIVE YOU THE MONEY AND PLENTY OF CREDIT.

I STARTED A FACTORY IN *BIELSKO*, AND VISITED TO ANJA EVERY WEEK-END.

BY OCTOBER 1937, THE FACTORY WAS GOING, AND IT WAS BORN MY FIRST SON, RICHIEU.

HE'S A BIG BABY- OVER 3 KILOS.

MY GOD. ANJA ONLY WEIGHS 39!

OF COURSE, YOU NEVER KNEW HIM. HE DIDN'T COME OUT FROM THE WAR.

YES, I KNOW...

BUT WAIT- IF YOU WERE MARRIED IN FEBRUARY, AND RICHIEU WAS BORN IN OCTOBER, WAS HE PREMATURE?

YES, A LITTLE...

BUT YOU-AFTER THE WAR, WHEN YOU WERE BORN- IT WAS VERY PREMATURE. THE DOCTORS THOUGHT YOU WOULDN'T LIVE.

I FOUND A SPECIALIST WHAT SAVED YOU... HE HAD TO BREAK YOUR ARM TO TAKE YOU OUT FROM ANJA'S BELLY!

AND WHEN YOU WERE A TINY BABY YOUR ARM ALWAYS JUMPED UP, LIKE SO!

WE JOKED AND CALLED YOU "HEIL HITLER!"

ALWAYS WE PUSHED YOUR ARM DOWN, AND YOU WOULD OOPS!

LOOK NOW WHAT YOU MADE ME DO!

ME? OKAY, I'LL RE-COUNT THEM LATER.

NO! YOU DON'T KNOW COUNTING PILLS. I'LL DO IT AFTER... I'M AN EXPERT FOR THIS.

SO... ANJA STAYED WITH THE FAMILY AND I WENT TO LIVE IN BIELSKO FOR MY FACTORY BUSINESS AND TO FIND FOR US AN APARTMENT...

BUT SOON IT CAME FROM SOSNOWIEC A TELEPHONE...

VLADEK? COME HOME RIGHT AWAY— ANJA IS *SICK!*

SHE WAS CRYING AS SOON I CAME IN...

WHAT'S WRONG, DARLING?

SOB
IT DOESN'T MATTER... *NOTHING* MATTERS.

BUT WHY ARE YOU CRYING?

I DON'T *KNOW!* I HAVE A GOOD FAMI-LY...A FINE SON...I SHOULD BE *HAPPY*...

BUT I DON'T CARE. I JUST DON'T WANT TO LIVE.

HERE, BABY. DRINK THIS AND REST.

I DON'T UNDERSTAND. WHAT'S THE MATTER?

GIVING BIRTH WAS TOO MUCH OF A STRAIN. SHE'S ALWAYS HYSTER-ICAL OR DEPRESSED...A *BREAKDOWN!*

PLEASE

THE DOCTOR TOLD US ABOUT A SANITARIUM.

...BUT SOMEBODY MUST GO WITH HER...SOMEONE SHE TRUSTS.

EVERYTHING'S ARRANGED—THE CHILD CAN STAY HERE WITH A GOVERNESS.

...AND I'LL WATCH YOUR FACTORY.

SOB

31

I TELL YOU, THERE'S A POGROM GOING ON IN GERMANY TODAY!

ONE FELLOW TOLD US OF HIS COUSIN WHAT WAS LIVING IN GERMANY...

...HE HAD TO SELL HIS BUSINESS TO A GERMAN AND RUN OUT FROM THE COUNTRY WITHOUT EVEN THE MONEY.

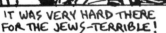

I AM A FILTHY JEW

IT WAS VERY HARD THERE FOR THE JEWS—TERRIBLE!

ANOTHER FELLOW TOLD US OF A RELATIVE IN BRANDENBERG—THE POLICE CAME TO HIS HOUSE AND NO ONE HEARD AGAIN FROM HIM.

This Town is Jew Free

IT WAS MANY, MANY SUCH STORIES—SYNAGOGUES BURNED, JEWS BEATEN WITH NO REASON, WHOLE TOWNS PUSHING OUT ALL JEWS—EACH STORY WORSE THAN THE OTHER.

LET'S HOPE THOSE NAZI GANGSTERS GET THROWN OUT OF POWER!

JUST PRAY THAT THEY DON'T START A WAR!!

33

THE SANITARIUM WAS FAR AWAY FROM EVERYTHING— SO PEACEFUL, SO QUIET.

LOOK AT HOW BEAUTIFUL THESE GARDENS ARE, ANJA.

UH HUH

PEOPLE CAME FROM ALL OVER THE WORLD WITH DIFFERENT SICKNESSES. IT WAS EVEN SHOPS HERE... A THEATER... REALLY BEAUTIFUL...

OUR ROOM IS LIKE A LUXURY HOTEL—LOOK AT THIS VIEW.

UH HUH

EACH MORNING NURSES WOULD VISIT TO ANJA.

AND EACH FEW DAYS I TALKED TO THE BIG SPECIALIST AT THE CLINIC.

WELL, WHAT DID THE DOCTOR SAY??

HE TOLD ME YOU'RE DOING FINE... FINE...

JUST RELAX.

I UNDERSTOOD MUCH OF SUCH SICKNESSES, SO I HELPED ALWAYS TO CALM HER DOWN.

LOOK—WE GOT A LETTER FROM HOME TODAY.

WITH A PHOTO OF RICHIEU—LET ME SEE.

HE'S A HANDSOME BOY... JUST LIKE HIS FATHER, YES?

YES.

IN THE EVENINGS WE WENT EITHER TO THE THEATER OR TO DANCE IN THE CAFE.

DID I TELL YOU THE TRAGEDY ABOUT THE PILLOW MY FAMILY LOST AT THE START OF THE 1914 WAR! I WAS SEVEN... WE LIVED TOO CLOSE TO THE BORDER... IT WASN'T SAFE...

I TOLD HER MANY JOKES AND STORIES TO KEEP HER BUSY...

...SO WE TOOK WHAT WE COULD ON A WAGON PULLED BY FOUR HORSES AND WENT TO MY GRANDFATHER'S HOME IN RADOMSKO.

SOMEONE RODE PAST US AND TOLD US THAT WE'D DROPPED A PILLOW A FEW MILES BACK. A GUY TRAVELING TO AMSTOW PICKED IT UP.

IMAGINE — MY FATHER NEVER RODE A HORSE BEFORE... BUT HE UNHITCHED ONE FROM THE WAGON AND RODE TOWARD AMSTOW..

WE WAITED AND WAITED.. MOTHER STARTED CRYING: "SURELY HE FELL AND GOT KILLED!" SHE HAD BEGGED HIM TO "LET THE PILLOW GO AND TAKE ALL OUR TROUBLES WITH IT!"

THE HORSE WAS BONY AND DIDN'T HAVE A SADDLE... FINALLY, LATE THAT NIGHT, FATHER RODE BACK WITH THE PILLOW ...UNDER HIS BLOODY "TUCHUS"...

SO, FATHER GOT HIS PILLOW BACK ...BUT HE COULDN'T SIT DOWN FOR THE REST OF THE WAR!

I LOVE YOU, VLADEK.

AND SHE WAS SO LAUGHING AND SO HAPPY, SO HAPPY, THAT SHE APPROACHED EACH TIME AND KISSED ME, SO HAPPY SHE WAS.

35

WE STAYED MAYBE 3 MONTHS, AND WHEN WE CAME BACK, ANJA WAS COMPLETELY DIFFERENT FROM WHEN SHE LEFT.

YOO HOO, POPPA!

ANJA! YOU LOOK LIKE A MILLION!

LISTEN, VLADEK... I DIDN'T WANT YOU TO WORRY WHILE YOU WERE AT THE SANITARIUM, BUT —

—BRACE YOURSELF—THE BIELSKO FACTORY HAS BEEN ROBBED!

WHAT!

IT HAPPENED LAST MONTH. THEY TOOK EVERYTHING!

AI! AI! AI!

I DIDN'T EVEN HAVE TIME TO INSURE IT BEFORE WE LEFT.

WELL, AT LEAST I CAN HELP YOU BUILD IT UP AGAIN.

WERE YOU LOOTED AS PART OF SOME KIND OF ANTI-SEMITIC ACTIVITY?

I DON'T THINK THIS WAS IT. JUST A ROBBERY...

...LIKE WHEN THEY ROBBED US IN REGO PARK HERE, LAST YEAR.

WELL.... IN BIELSKO, FATHER-IN-LAW HELPED US AGAIN TO ESTABLISH OURSELVES ...

IN A COUPLE MONTHS WE WERE WELL-OFF— QUITE WELL-OFF... A WORKING FACTORY, A 2 BEDROOM APARTMENT, A POLISH GOVERNESS, AND EVEN A MAID.

LOOK, RICHIEU, POPPA'S HOME!

YOU LOOK UPSET, VLADEK.

THERE WAS ANOTHER RIOT DOWNTOWN TODAY.

...EVERYONE YELLING, "JEWS OUT! JEWS OUT!"... EVEN TWO PEOPLE KILLED. THE POLICE JUST WATCHED!

IT'S THOSE NAZIS STIRRING EVERYBODY UP!

WHEN IT COMES TO JEWS, THE POLES DON'T NEED MUCH STIRRING UP!

MRS. SPIEGELMAN— HOW CAN YOU SAY SUCH A THING. I THINK OF YOU AS PART OF MY OWN FAMILY!

I'M SORRY, JANINA. I DIDN'T MEAN YOU! I'M JUST WORRIED!

MAYBE WE SHOULD MOVE AWAY, LIKE SOME OTHERS HAVE.

IF THINGS GET REALLY BAD WE'LL RUN BACK TO SOSNOWIEC.

WHY WOULD SOSNOWIEC BE ANY SAFER THAN BIELSKO?

WE THOUGHT THEN, THAT HITLER WANTED ONLY THE PARTS FROM POLAND, LIKE BIELSKO, WHAT USED TO BE PARTS FROM GERMANY BEFORE THE FIRST WORLD WAR.

WE WERE VERY HAPPY, STILL, FOR OVER A YEAR—UNTIL AUGUST 24, 1939.

A LETTER—FROM THE GOVERNMENT!

A DRAFT NOTICE! I WAS IN THE POLISH RESERVES ARMY, AND SO I HAD TO GO RIGHT AWAY!

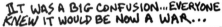

IT WAS A BIG CONFUSION... EVERYONE KNEW IT WOULD BE NOW A WAR...

QUICK! PACK EVERYTHING! YOUR FATHER WILL TAKE YOU TO SOSNOWIEC.

VLADEK, I'M AFRAID!

GRAB YOUR KNICK-KNACKS, AND THE DOLL COLLECTION!

THEY'RE NOT IMPORTANT!

YOU'LL SEE. YOU MAY ENJOY THEM.

I WAS RIGHT. WHEN THINGS WENT WORSE LATER, SHE WAS ABLE TO SELL SUCH THINGS.

SO ANJA AND RICHIEU AND THE GOVERNESS WENT IN ONE WAY—TO SOSNOWIEC...

...AND I WENT THEN IN A DIFFERENT DIRECTION...TO THE FRONTIER AGAINST GERMANY.

..AND ON SEPTEMBER 1, 1939, THE WAR CAME. I WAS ON THE FRONT, ONE OF THE FIRST TO *ACH!*

SO..TWICE I SPILLED MY DRUGSTORE!

IT'S MY EYES.

EVER SINCE I GOT IN MY LEFT EYE THE HEMORRHAGING AND THE GLAUCOMA, IT HAD TO BE TAKEN OUT FROM ME. AND NOW I DON'T SEE SO WELL.

AND NOW I HAVE A **CATARACT** INSIDE MY ONE GOOD EYE. YOU SEE HOW I HAVE TO SUFFER?

I TOLD YOU ABOUT THE BIG-SHOT SPECIALIST WHAT WAS GOING TO OPERATE ME?

UH-HUH.

HE LAST YEAR PUT ME INTO THE HOSPITAL FOR AN IMMEDIATE OPERATION...

AND THEN HE JUST **LEFT** ME.. HE WENT SOMEWHERE AWAY TO GIVE LECTURES ON THE TELEVISION!

MY EYE STARTED SO **BLEEDING**, I HAD TO RUN OUT TO FIND A DOCTOR IN A DIFFERENT HOSPITAL.

THERE ANOTHER SPECIALIST OPERATED RIGHT **AWAY!** OTHERWISE I COULD HAVE DIED.

SO NOW ITS A **GLASS EYE.**

HE DID A GOOD JOB, NO? ONE TIME, EVEN, A YOUNG DOCTOR CAME TO MY BED THERE IN THE HOSPITAL...

HE LOOKED WITH A LIGHT A LONG TIME IN MY EYES AND TOLD: "MR. SPIEGELMAN, YOUR LEFT EYE IS **PERFECT!**..

"...BUT IN YOUR **RIGHT** EYE IS **CATARACTS.**"

HE DIDN'T KNOW, OF COURSE, THAT THE LEFT EYE IS GLASS...

AND I DIDN'T TELL ANYTHING TO HIM. I DIDN'T WANT TO MAKE HIM AN EMBARRASSMENT.

UH-HUH. YOU TOLD ME ABOUT THAT.

WELL, IT'S ENOUGH FOR TODAY, YES? I'M TIRED AND I MUST COUNT STILL MY PILLS.

OKAY, GOOD IDEA... MY HAND IS SORE FROM WRITING ALL THIS DOWN.

CHAPTER THREE

I visited my father more often in order to get more information about his past..

HAVE SOME MORE GREEN BEANS, ARTIE.

YES, LOOK - YOU DON'T EAT ANYTHING!

NO THANKS. I'VE HAD ENOUGH.

SO FINISH AT LEAST WHAT'S ON YOUR PLATE!

OKAY... OKAY.

Y'KNOW, MALA, WHEN I WAS LITTLE, IF I DIDN'T EAT EVERYTHING MOM SERVED, POP AND I WOULD ARGUE 'TIL I RAN TO MY ROOM CRYING ...

YOU SHOULD KNOW IT'S IMPOSSIBLE TO ARGUE WITH YOUR FATHER.

...MOM WOULD OFFER TO COOK SOMETHING I LIKED BETTER, BUT POP JUST WANTED TO LEAVE THE LEFT-OVER FOOD AROUND UNTIL I ATE IT.

SOMETIMES HE'D EVEN SAVE IT TO SERVE AGAIN AND AGAIN UNTIL I'D EAT IT OR STARVE.

YES! SO IT HAS TO BE. ALWAYS YOU MUST EAT ALL WHAT IS ON YOUR PLATE.

ACCH, VLADEK.

43

FORTUNATELY FOR ME, MOM WOULD EVENTUALLY FEED ME SOMETHING I LIKED, AND THROW AWAY THE OLD FOOD WHILE YOU WEREN'T LOOKING.

YES. ANJA WAS TOO EASY WITH YOU ALWAYS.

HMMH. THANKS FOR THE DINNER, MALA. IT WAS DELICIOUS.

PFEH – THE CHICKEN WAS, I THOUGHT, TOO DRY. COME, WE'LL TALK BETTER IN THE LIVING ROOM.

OKAY – I'LL GET MY NOTEBOOK.

...I TELL YOU, WITH MALA I DON'T KNOW WHAT TO DO. SHE—

PLEASE, POP! I'D RATHER NOT HEAR ALL THAT AGAIN. TELL ME ABOUT 1939, WHEN YOU WERE DRAFTED.

1939? YES...WE WERE GIVEN ARMY TRAININGS FOR A FEW DAYS AND THEN, BY THE START OF SEPTEMBER WE WERE ON THE FRONTIER.

...WE WERE ALL DIGGED INTO TRENCHES NEAR A RIVER. ON THE OTHER SIDE IT WAS GERMANS.

44

THREE MONTHS BEFORE THE EXAMINATION HE STARTED WITH ME...

WAKE UP, VLADEK!

YOU'RE SLEEPING TOO MUCH!

ONLY THREE HOURS A NIGHT?

STOP, VLADEK. YOU MUSTN'T EAT SO MUCH!

BUT I'M HUNGRY!

OKAY— HAVE ONE MORE HERRING.

FOR THREE MONTHS I ATE ONLY SALTED HERRING AND NO WATER TO LOSE WEIGHT.

AND A FEW DAYS BEFORE THE EXAM, *NO* SLEEP AND *NO* FOOD...

GOOD BOY—JUST A LITTLE MORE COFFEE!

ONLY A GALLON COFFEE A DAY FOR MY HEART.

AND WHEN FINALLY I WENT FOR MY MEDICAL EXAMINATION...

HERE'S A HEALTHY ONE.

UM!...

NO...THERE SEEMS TO BE *SOMETHING* WRONG WITH HIM.

BUILD YOURSELF UP FOR A YEAR, YOUNG MAN, AND WE'LL REVIEW YOUR CASE AGAIN.

46

...THE NEXT YEAR FATHER WANTED I WOULD **AGAIN** DO THE SAME THING. BUT I BEGGED HIM AND AT 22 WENT INTO THE ARMY...

BUT LET'S GET BACK TO 1939!

YES. YOU SEE HOW YOU MIX ME UP? ...IN 1939 WE WERE ON THE FRONTIER, DIGGED INTO TRENCHES BY A RIVER.

IT WAS QUIET UNTIL NEAR MORNING. THEN I HEARD SHOOTING ON BOTH SIDES.

AN OFFICER SNEAKED OVER TO ME.

DIG IN DEEPER. YOU'LL GET KILLED.

YOUR GUN IS COLD! WHY AREN'T YOU SHOOTING?

I DIDN'T SEE AT **WHAT** TO SHOOT...

KPOK! KPOK! KPOK!

...BUT I DIGGED DEEPER AND STARTED TO SHOOT!

THEN BULLETS CAME IN MY DIRECTION.

I DUG DEEPER MY TRENCH BUT I STOPPED TO SHOOT.

BUT WHEN I LOOKED IN MY GUN, I SAW... A TREE!///

AND THE TREE WAS ACTUALLY MOVING!

WELL, IF IT MOVED, I HAD TO SHOOT!

IT HELD UP A HAND TO SHOW IT WAS HURT. TO SURRENDER.

BUT I KEPT SHOOTING AND SHOOTING. UNTIL FINALLY THE TREE STOPPED MOVING. WHO KNOWS; OTHERWISE HE COULD HAVE SHOT ME!

48

ANOTHER GERMAN TOOK 4 OR 5 FROM US TO A STABLE.

SEE THIS MESS? IT BETTER BE SPOTLESSLY CLEAN IN ONE HOUR. UNDERSTAND!

IT WAS IMPOSSIBLE TO DO IT IN ONE HOUR!

WE REALLY WORKED VERY HARD. BUT, AN HOUR LATER...

SO!

NOT FINISHED YET?

THIS WILL COST YOU YOUR SOUP, YOU LAZY BASTARDS!

AND SOMEHOW WE DID MAKE THE JOB IN ONLY AN HOUR AND A HALF. BUT LOOK WHAT YOU DO, ARTIE!

HUH?

YOU'RE DROPPING ON THE CARPET CIGARETTE ASHES. YOU WANT IT SHOULD BE LIKE A STABLE HERE?

OOPS. SORRY.

CLEAN IT, YES? OTHERWISE I HAVE TO DO IT. MALA COULD LET IT SIT LIKE THIS FOR A WEEK AND NEVER TOUCH IT.

AND SHE KNOWS HOW WITH MY SICKNESSES IT'S HARD NOW FOR ME TO DO SUCH THINGS.

OKAY, OKAY. IT'S CLEAN.

52

SO WE LIVED AND WORKED A FEW WEEKS IN THE STABLE UNTIL THEY TOOK US TO AN EVEN *BIGGER* PRISONER OF WAR CAMP.

BRRR. THE POLISH PRISONERS GET *HEATED* CABINS.

YES, AND WE'RE JUST LEFT TO FREEZE IN THESE TENTS.

IT WAS TERRIBLE COLD THAT AUTUMN. ALL OVER EUROPE IT WAS SO FREEZING THAT BIRDS FELL FROM TREES.

TO KEEP WARM WE HAD ONLY OUR SUMMER UNIFORMS AND A THIN BLANKET.

AT LEAST IF THEY GAVE US ENOUGH TO EAT.

THE OTHER PRISONERS GET *TWO* MEALS A DAY. WE JEWS GET ONLY A CRUST OF BREAD AND A LITTLE SOUP.

GOOD MORNING, VLADEK.

WHERE ARE YOU GOING?

TO BATHE IN THE RIVER.

YOU'VE GONE CRAZY.

BRR. I'LL BE *CLEAN!* AND I'LL FEEL WARM ALL DAY BY COMPARISON.

MANY OTHERS GOT FROSTBITE WOUNDS. IN THE WOUNDS WAS PUS, AND IN THE PUS WAS LICE.

EVERY DAY I BATHED AND DID GYMNASTICS TO KEEP STRONG ...AND EVERY DAY WE PRAYED.

I WAS VERY RELIGIOUS, AND IT WASN'T *ELSE* TO DO.

OFTEN WE PLAYED CHESS TO KEEP OUR MINDS BUSY AND MAKE THE TIME GO.

I HAD A SET MADE FROM STONES AND BREAD CRUMBS.

AND ONE TIME A WEEK WE COULD WRITE LETTERS THROUGH THE INTERNATIONAL RED CROSS.

Dear Anja. I am fine. I miss you.

ONLY IN GERMAN. AND VERY CAREFUL.

AND THROUGH THIS IT CAME A PACKAGE...

CHOCOLATE BARS! CIGARETTES! JAM!

IT WAS SO TREASURING FOR ME THIS PACKAGE.

I HAD A SIGN MY FAMILY WAS SAFE, AND— BECAUSE I NEVER SMOKED—I HAD CIGARETTES TO TRADE FOR FOOD.

AND SO THINGS WENT FOR MAYBE SIX WEEKS, THEN...

LOOK! THERE'S AN ANNOUNCE- MENT OUTSIDE!

WORKERS NEEDED
War Prisoners may volun- teer for labor assignments to replace German work- ers called to the front. Housing and abundant food will be supplied.

IT'S A TRICK!

NEVER VOLUNTEER! IF WE *HAVE* TO DIE, LET'S DIE *HERE*!

NO!

I DIDN'T AGREE!

I'M NOT GOING TO DIE, AND I WON'T DIE HERE! I WANT TO BE TREATED LIKE A HUMAN BEING!

WHEN MY COMRADES SAW I WAS GOING, THEY TOO REGISTERED.

WE WERE RIGHT AWAY SENT TO A BIG GERMAN COMPANY.

WE WERE TAKEN TO NICE WOODEN HOUSES. WE GOT SOUP AND WE GOT BREAD...

LOOK! A STOVE!

AND REAL BEDS!

WITH SHEETS AND PILLOWS!

AND FOR A WHOLE DAY WE ONLY RESTED AND GOT BACK OUR STRENGTH.

AH- IT SEEMS LIKE YEARS SINCE I'VE FELT WARM OR BEEN IN A BED!

YES- FUNNY, ISN'T IT? IT'S ONLY A LITTLE OVER 2 MONTHS SINCE WE WERE DRAFTED.

I'M WORRIED THOUGH, VLADEK- WHO KNOWS WHAT KIND OF WORK THEY'LL GIVE US.

IT DOESN'T MATTER..

..ANYTHING IS BETTER THAN ROTTING IN THOSE TENTS.

I SUPPOSE.

THE NEXT DAY WE WERE GIVEN SHOVELS AND PICKS ...

...THINGS WHAT WE NEVER HELD IN OUR HANDS BEFORE.

AND THE WORK WAS REALLY VERY HARD—
WE HAD TO MOVE MOUNTAINS.

MOUNTAIN

VALLEY

THE HILLS WERE MAYBE
3 OR 4 YARDS HIGH. WE
HAD TO MAKE IT LEVEL.

SOME COMPLAINED—THOSE WHAT WERE
TOO OLD OR WEAK FOR SUCH WORK:

I—I CANT TAKE
ANYMORE.

WORTHLESS
JEW!

IF YOU'RE UNHAPPY—GO BACK
TO THE P.O.W. CAMP.

IT'S OKAY—WE'LL HELP YOU
WHEN NO ONE IS LOOKING.

WE TRIED TO HELP, BUT—WHAT YOU
THINK?—SOME WENT BACK TO THE
TENTS TO FREEZE AND TO STARVE.

BUT WHAT HAP-
PENED TO THEM,
I DON'T KNOW.

STILL, EIGHTY PER CENT STAYED. THERE WAS ENOUGH
TO EAT, AND A WARM BED. IT WAS BETTER TO STAY...

SO WE WORKED, DAY AFTER DAY. WE SURVIVED. WEEK AFTER WEEK. THE SAME.

UNTIL, ONE TIME...

LOOK - SOLDIERS!

IT CAME VERY MANY GESTAPO AND WEHRMACHT.

ATTENTION! LINE UP ON THE ROAD IN TWO ROWS! IMMEDIATELY!

WE WERE NOT AT EASE. WE DIDN'T KNOW WHAT THEY COULD DO WITH US.

I STOOD ALWAYS IN THE SECOND LINE.

(PSST - VLADEK.)

I DIDN'T WANT THEY SHOULD SEE ME MUCH.

SOMEONE SNEAKED NEXT TO ME...

RABBI! DO YOU KNOW WHAT DAY IT IS?

SATURDAY, OF COURSE.

BUT DO YOU KNOW WHAT A SATURDAY?...

IT'S PARSHAS TRUMA!

58

THEY MARCHED US TO THE MAIN COURTYARD AND LINED US BY ALPHABET AT TABLES...

NAME AND RANK?

SPIEGELMAN, VLADEK. CORPORAL.

DESTINATION UPON RELEASE?

SOSNOWIEC...

THIS THE GERMANS DID VERY GOOD...

...TO MY WIFE AND CHILD.

...ALWAYS THEY DID EVERYTHING VERY SYSTEMATIC.

VERY WELL- SIGN THIS RELEASE FORM.

...AND IT WAS ALL DONE IN ONE DAY.

YOU MEAN YOUR 'PARSHAS TRUMA' DREAM ACTUALLY CAME TRUE?

YES-THIS IS FOR ME A VERY IMPORTANT DATE...

I CHECKED LATER ON A CALENDAR. IT WAS THIS PARSHA ON THE WEEK I GOT MARRIED TO ANJA.

...AND THIS WAS THE PARSHA IN 1948, AFTER THE WAR, ON THE WEEK YOU WERE BORN!...

AND SO IT CAME OUT TO BE THIS PARSHA YOU SANG ON THE SATURDAY OF YOUR BAR MITZVAH!

THE NEXT MORNING EACH FROM US GOT A RED CROSS PACKAGE, AND THEY LOADED US ON A TRAIN TO POLAND.

DURING THE JOURNEY I SAT WITH THE RABBI.

SO, MY SON. NOW I SEE YOU ARE A "ROH-EH HANOLED," ONE WHO SEES WHAT THE FUTURE WILL BRING.

HEY! THIS TRAIN SEEMS TO BE PASSING SOSNOWIEC!

WHEN THEY DIDN'T STOP THE TRAIN I BECAME VERY WORRIED.

YOU SEE, THE NAZIS DIVIDED POLAND INTO PIECES: PROTECTORATE and REICH, WITH A GUARDED BORDER BETWEEN.

BALTIC SEA
LITHUANIA
E. PRUSSIA
(annexed to Russia)
GERMANY
POLAND
SOVIET UNION
WARSAW
LUBLIN
SOSNOWIEC
KRAKOW
HUNGARY
SLOVAKIA
RUMANIA

REICH: Annexed to Germany.
PROTECTORATE: German controlled Government.

THE TRAIN WENT COMPLETELY PAST MY PART OF POLAND—THE REICH—AND STOPPED ONLY IN THE PROTECTORATE.

THOSE WITH PAPERS FOR KRAKOW-OUT!

AND, WHEN IT STOPPED IN WARSAW, THE RABBI GOT OUT.

I'LL WRITE TO YOU.

BUT I NEVER HEARD AGAIN FROM HIM. IT CAME SUCH A MISERY IN WARSAW, ALMOST NONE SURVIVED.

AND THE TRAIN WAS A LONG WAY PAST SOSNOWIEC. THEY TOOK ME UP, UP, VERY FAR—MAYBE 300 MILES—UNTIL WE CAME TO LUBLIN. THERE THEY UNLOADED ALL OF US FROM THE REICH.

60

IN LUBLIN, THEY TOOK US TO BIG TENTS...

AND THERE WE SAT.

EVENTUALLY CAME SOME PEOPLE TO SEE US FROM THE JEWISH AUTHORITIES...

WHY ARE WE BEING KEPT HERE?

IT'S A VERY BAD SITUATION... JUST BEFORE YOU ARRIVED, THERE WAS ANOTHER GROUP OF RELEASED WAR PRISONERS...

...TWO DAYS AGO THE NAZIS MARCHED THEM TO A FOREST,....

...AND THEY SHOT ALL OF THEM—THEY KILLED 600 PEOPLE!

WE WERE THE NEXT PARTY!

I THOUGHT YOU WERE *RELEASED* AS A PRISONER OF WAR!

EXACTLY SO..

INTERNATIONAL LAWS PROTECTED US A LITTLE AS POLISH WAR PRISONERS. BUT A JEW OF THE REICH, ANYONE COULD KILL IN THE STREETS!

I WAS VERY FRIGHTENED.

THEN WE HEARD SOMETHING TO GIVE US A LITTLE HOPE....

WE'VE BRIBED THE GERMANS TO RELEASE PRISONERS INTO THE HOMES OF LOCAL JEWS WHO WILL CLAIM YOU AS RELATIVES.

MY NAME'S SPIEGELMAN. THERE'S A FRIEND OF MY FAMILY NAMED ORBACH IN LUBLIN. I MET HIM WHEN I WAS HERE FOR ARMY TRAINING.

FINE! WE'LL TRY TO REGISTER YOU AS HIS COUSIN.

THAT NIGHT I WENT OUT FROM THE TENT...

I HAD TO URINATE.

I RAN QUICK INSIDE ....

AND THOUGHT ALL NIGHT DIFFERENT THINGS WHAT COULD HAPPEN TO US.

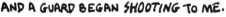

AND A GUARD BEGAN *SHOOTING* TO ME.

THEN, AS SOON AS IT WAS LIGHT:

SPIEGELMAN!.. SPIEGELMAN!..

VLADEK!

ORBACH! AM I GLAD TO SEE YOU!

AND IN TEN MINUTES, I WAS FREE!

ORBACH WAS A FRIEND FROM MY UNCLE - HE HAD TWO BEAUTIFUL DAUGHTERS NEAR TO MY AGE.

I'M SORRY WE CAN'T OFFER YOU A BETTER MEAL, VLADEK - BUT THE JEWS OF LUBLIN GET VERY FEW FOOD COUPONS.

ONE MOMENT, GIRLS - I HAVE A GIFT FOR EACH OF YOU...

OH MY GOD! CHOCOLATE!

THESE I SAVED FROM A RED CROSS PACKAGE. ALWAYS I SAVED... JUST IN CASE!

EVENTUALLY, WHEN I CAME AGAIN TO SOSNOWIEC, WE SENT THEM FOOD PACKAGES...

... WE WERE FOR A WHILE A LITTLE BETTER OFF... AND THEY WROTE BACK VERY HAPPY HOW IT HELPED SURVIVE THEM...

...THEN THEY WROTE THAT THE GERMANS WERE KEEPING THE PACKAGES. AND THEN THEY STOPPED TO WRITE. FINISHED.

WITH ORBACHS' I STAYED A FEW DAYS RECUPERATING. BUT I WAS RESTLESS. HOW COULD I MANAGE TO SNEAK ACROSS THE BORDER TO MY FAMILY?

63

TRAINS WERE STILL GOING FROM PROTECTORATE TO REICH. ONLY, ONE NEEDED LEGAL PAPERS. OF COURSE, THIS I DIDN'T HAVE ...

...BUT ANYWAY I GOT ON THE TRAIN IN THE DIRECTION I WANTED.

I APPROACHED TO THE TRAIN MAN, A POLE...

MAY I TALK TO YOU FOR A MOMENT?

SURE, SOLDIER.

I STILL HAD ON MY ARMY UNIFORM, AND I DIDN'T LET KNOW I WAS A JEW.

YOU'RE A POLE LIKE ME, SO I CAN TRUST YOU ... THE STINKING NAZIS HAD ME IN A WAR PRISON ... I JUST ESCAPED.

THE POLES WERE VERY BITTER ON THE GERMANS, SO IT WAS GOOD TO SPEAK BAD OF THEM.

I'M TRYING TO GET TO SOSNOWIEC — BACK TO MY FAMILY.

DON'T WORRY ... WHEN WE GET TO THE BORDER, HIDE IN HERE.

AND SO THE TRAIN MAN HELPED ME COME BACK TO MY SIDE OF POLAND.

...WHAT I THOUGHT I MIGHT NEVER SEE AGAIN.

OY GEVALT! IT'S VLADEK!

I WALKED FIRST OVER TO MY PARENTS' HOUSE...

64

MY SON! THANK GOD YOU'RE SAFE! AND IN SPITE OF EVERYTHING, YOU LOOK *HEALTHY*!

I'M STRONG, MOTHER. BUT *YOU* LOOK SICK! IT'S BECAUSE I WAS WORRIED ABOUT YOU.

BUT IT WASN'T ONLY THIS. SHE WAS SICK OF CANCER.

...AND A MONTH OR TWO LATER, SHE DIED. SHE NEVER KNEW HOW TERRIBLE EVERYTHING WOULD SOON BE!

-AND, FATHER! YOUR BEARD! WHAT HAPPENED? YOU *SHAVED* IT OFF?!?? IT'S GROWING BACK, NOW...

HE WAS VERY RELIGIOUS - SO LIKE A RABBI - AND, OF COURSE, HE ALWAYS HAD A BIG BEARD.

IN SEPTEMBER THE GERMAN SOLDIERS GRABBED MANY JEWS IN THE STREET...

THEY MADE US SING PRAYERS WHILE THEY LAUGHED AND BEAT US.

...AND BEFORE LETTING US GO, THEY CUT OFF OUR BEARDS.

AND NOW THE DEMONS HAVE TAKEN AWAY MY SELTZER FACTORY. THEY—

ENOUGH!

I MUST BRING VLADEK HOME TO ANJA BEFORE CURFEW.

AT 7:00 IT WAS A RULE. ALL JEWS HAD TO BE IN THEIR HOME. AND ALL LIGHTS OUT.

FROM MY PARENTS' TO SOSNOWIEC WAS ONLY A SHORT RIDE.

GO IN AND SAY YOU JUST GOT A LETTER FROM ME SAYING I'D BE HOME IN A WEEK.

I STOOD AT THE DOOR, LISTENING...

DON'T JOKE! IF VLADEK WAS COMING HOME, HE'D HAVE WRITTEN TO US TOO!

SURPRISE!

OH MY GOD.

VLADEK!

I GRABBED MY SON. HE WAS 2½ YEARS.

RICHIEU!

BWAAH

HE STARTED SCREAMING.

WHY DO YOU CRY, MY BOY? I'M YOUR FATHER!

WAH

˸SNF˸ TH' BUTTONS. YOUR METAL BUTTONS, DADDY—THEY'RE COLD!

AND I DON'T NEED TO TELL YOU HOW BIG THE JOY WAS IN OUR HOUSE.

66

CHAPTER FOUR

WHEN FIRST I CAME HOME IT LOOKED EXACTLY SO AS BEFORE I WENT AWAY...

IT WAS STILL VERY LUXURIOUS. THE GERMANS COULDN'T DESTROY EVERYTHING AT ONE TIME.

IT WAS TWELVE OF US LIVING IN FATHER-IN-LAW'S HOUSEHOLD...

IT WAS ANJA AND ME, AND OUR BOY, RICHIEU...

ANJA'S OLDER SISTER, TOSHA, HER HUSBAND, WOLFE, AND THEIR LITTLE GIRL, BIBI...

AND IT WAS ANJA'S GRANDPARENTS. THEY HAD MAYBE 90 YEARS, BUT VERY ALERT...

AND, OF COURSE, IT WAS MY FATHER-IN-LAW AND MY MOTHER-IN-LAW...

AND ALSO THE 2 KIDS FROM YOUR UNCLE HERMAN AND AUNT HELEN: LOLEK AND LONIA

HERMAN AND HELA WERE LUCKY. THEY WERE VISITING THE N.Y. WORLD'S FAIR WHEN THE WAR CAME

THIS SAVED THEM.

WELL, WE SHOULD BE HAPPY WE'RE ALL TOGETHER WITH ENOUGH TO EAT.

BUT WE MUST REALLY TIGHTEN OUR BELTS UNTIL THE WAR ENDS.

COME—LET'S PLAY RUMMY WHILE THE LADIES CLEAR THE TABLE.

HAS THE FAMILY BEEN TAKING GOOD CARE OF MY BIELSKO TEXTILE FACTORY?

DON'T YOU KNOW? ..ALL JEWISH BUS-INESSES HAVE BEEN TAKEN OVER BY "ARYAN MANAGERS"..

I WENT TO OUR FACTORY IN LODZ, AND THEY SAID, "BETTER GO HOME TODAY, OLD MAN...TOMORROW WE'LL CARRY YOU OUT.

WHAT?

BUT ISN'T ANY MONEY COMING IN?

NOT A SINGLE ZLOTY. AND THE FAMILY WANTS TO LIVE THE WAY IT DID BEFORE THE WAR!

OKAY, VLADEK—CUT THE CARDS.

BUT, WOLFE—WHAT KIND OF WORK ARE *YOU* DOING?

JUST A LITTLE OFFICE WORK FOR THE GEMEINDE ... BUT A FEW MONTHS AGO FATHER-IN-LAW TOOK ALL HIS VALUA-BLES HOME FROM THE BANK SAFE.

HOW LONG CAN SAVINGS LAST?

DON'T WORRY SO MUCH, VLADEK. YOU'LL SEE ... THE WAR WILL BE OVER LIKE LIGHTNING!

JA! LIKE LIGHTNING!

ACH!

WOLFE LOOKED ONLY TO PLAY CARDS.

I WENT THE NEXT DAY TO MODRZEJOWSKA STREET. HERE PEOPLE STILL MADE MONEY, FROM *SECRET* BUSINESSES... NOT SO LEGAL...

(PSST—FOOD COUPONS FOR REICHSMARKS?)

VLADEK SPIEGELMAN!

MR. ILZECKI! WHAT ARE YOU DOING IN SOSNOWIEC?

ILZECKI USED TO BE A CUSTOMER OF MINE. THE BEST TAILOR IN KATOWICE.

THE NAZIS MOVED ME TO AN APARTMENT HERE. I MAKE UNIFORMS FOR THEIR OFFICERS... AND SUITS ON THE SIDE WHEN I CAN GET THE CLOTH.

ARE YOU STILL IN BUSINESS?

I DON'T KNOW. I *JUST* GOT BACK FROM WAR PRISON.

WELL, IF YOU GET ANY CLOTH, COME SEE ME. THIS NOTE WILL GET YOU PAST THE DOORMAN.

THE NOTE TOLD THAT I WORKED WITH HIM. SUCH A PAPER COULD BE USEFUL TO HAVE.

I WENT THEN TO SHOPS WHAT STILL OWED ME MONEY FROM BEFORE THE WAR...

BUT I CAN'T PAY YOU! A GERMAN RUNS MY PLACE NOW. I'M LUCKY JUST TO HAVE A JOB!

THEN ADVANCE ME A FEW YARDS OF MATERIAL WITHOUT COUPONS.

OKAY, OKAY. HIDE THIS UNDER YOUR CLOTHES.

MR. ILZECKI, PLEASE.

SO I MADE A NICE FEW ZLOTYS THE VERY FIRST WEEK I CAME HOME.

I REMEMBER, FATHER-IN-LAW WAS SO HAPPY WITH ME.

YOU SEE, AT LEAST THERE'S ONE SMART GUY IN THE FAMILY.

OF COURSE I ONLY SAID I GOT *HALF* WHAT I REALLY MADE. OTHERWISE THEY WOULDN'T SAVE ANYTHING.

A LITTLE LATER I WAS AGAIN ON MODRZEJOWSKA, LOOKING TO BUY SOME TEXTILES WITHOUT COUPONS...

...THE S.S. CLOSED OFF THE WHOLE STREET TO INSPECT THE WORKING PAPERS FROM EVERYONE.

I DIDN'T *KNOW* BEFORE ABOUT THIS.

I MANAGED TO DISAPPEAR INTO A BUILDING.

BUT THEY TOOK MAYBE 50% OF THE PEOPLE AWAY.

I TALKED ABOUT IT TO FATHER-IN-LAW...

THEY ALMOST GOT ME! I'LL NEED MORE THAN JUST ILZECKI'S NOTE!

IT'S TRUE.

COME... WE'LL VISIT A FRIEND OF MINE WHO OWNS A TIN SHOP. I THINK HIS OVERSEER CAN BE BRIBED.

AND SO IT WENT...

OKAY, VLADEK... SINCE WE MAKE THINGS FOR GERMANY WE CAN GET YOU A PRIORITY WORK CARD.

REMEMBER, IF THERE'S A ROUND-UP, RUN IN HERE AND PRETEND YOU'RE WORKING.

I LEARNED HERE TO DO THINGS WHAT WERE USEFUL TO ME WHEN I CAME TO AUSCHWITZ.

AND SO WE LIVED FOR MORE THAN A YEAR. BUT ALWAYS THINGS CAME A LITTLE WORSE, A LITTLE WORSE...

FATHER-IN-LAW HAD A NICE NEW BEDROOM SET...

THE GERMANS *LOOKED* TO *GRAB* SUCH FURNITURE, BECAUSE IN STORES IT WASN'T ANYMORE TO GET.

WOLFE AND I SHLEPPED EVERYTHING VALUABLE DOWNSTAIRS FOR A POLISH NEIGHBOR TO HIDE.

OOF. ARE WE LEAVING THE OTHER BED UPSTAIRS?

JA. MOTHER-IN-LAW IS TOO SICK. SHE NEEDS A GOOD BED.

ANJA'S MOTHER HAD GALLSTONES. THE DAY THE GERMANS CAME SHE LAY IN THE BED.

PLEASE DON'T TAKE HER BED - LOOK AT HOW SICK SHE IS.

THE DOCTOR IS HERE EVERY DAY.

FATHER-IN-LAW HAD AN OLD FRIEND WHO CAME ALWAYS OVER TO PLAY CARDS.

...AND THEY LEFT WITHOUT TAKING *ANYTHING!*

YOU KNOW, I MET A GERMAN OFFICIAL WHO WOULD PAY WELL FOR A BEDROOM SET...

HIDDEN, WE HAD NO USE FROM THE FURNITURE. SO WE SHLEPPED IT AGAIN UPSTAIRS TO SELL.

YOU HAVE EXCELLENT TASTE IN FURNITURE, HERR ZYLBERBERG. THANK YOU.

MY MEN WILL BE RIGHT BACK TO GET YOUR *WIFE'S* BED TOO!...

YOU *CHEATED* US LAST TIME, JEW!

WAIT! I HAVEN'T BEEN PAID, YET.

PLEASE, IF YOU WANT TO STAY ALIVE GO BACK INSIDE.

HE WAS SO UNHAPPY AFTER. SO UNHAPPY!

ONE TIME I WAS GOING TO SEE ILZECKI. THIS WAS LATE IN 1941, I THINK. HIS HOUSE WAS VERY NEAR TO A TRAIN STATION...

... AND IT WAS GOING ON THERE SOMETHING **TERRIBLE.**

I HAD TO PASS NEAR— AND THEY WERE GRABBING JEWS, IF THEY HAD PAPERS OR NO!

WHAT HAD I TO DO?

WILL I WALK **SLOWLY, THEY** WILL **TAKE ME...**

WILL I **RUN** THEY CAN SHOOT ME!

THEN FROM FAR, I SAW ILZECKI WALKING, SO I WENT HASTY OVER TO HIM.

ALLO! MR. SPIEGELMAN! WHAT ARE YOU DOING HERE? DON'T YOU SEE WHAT'S GOING ON?

QUICK—COME UPSTAIRS WITH ME UNTIL THE TRAINS LEAVE!

ILZECKI LIVED IN A VERY FANCY HOUSE. HE WAS THE ONLY JEW THERE.

SO I SAT WITH HIM AND HIS WIFE A GOOD FEW HOURS. WE HEARD SHOOTING AND SCREAMS.

HE SURVIVED ME MY LIFE THAT TIME.

ILZECKI HAD A SON THE SAME AGE LIKE RICHIEU. IF YOU ONLY COULD SEE HOW THOSE CHILDREN PLAYED TOGETHER.

LISTEN, VLADEK..

WE CAN'T KNOW WHAT'S GOING TO HAPPEN TO *US* — BUT WE *MUST* KEEP OUR CHILDREN SAFE.

I HAVE A GOOD FRIEND, A POLE, WHO'S WILLING TO HIDE MY SON UNTIL THE SITUATION GETS BETTER.

...I THINK HE'D TAKE YOUR BOY TOO.

YES, YOU MAY BE RIGHT. LET ME SPEAK WITH MY FAMILY.

BUT, I'M TELLING YOU, IT WAS SOMETHING *TERRIBLE* GOING ON IN OUR HOUSE WHEN I EVEN *MENTIONED* IT.

WHAT? HAVE YOU GONE *CRAZY*?

HOW CAN YOU EVEN *THINK* OF GIVING RICHIEU UP TO COMPLETE STRANGERS?!

I'LL *NEVER* GIVE UP MY BABY. *NEVER!*

ILZECKI AND HIS WIFE DIDN'T COME OUT FROM THE WAR.

...BUT HIS SON REMAINED ALIVE; OURS DID NOT.

...AND *ANYWAY* WE HAD TO GIVE RICHIEU TO HIDE A YEAR LATER.

WHEN WE WERE IN THE GHETTO, IN 1943, TOSHA TOOK ALL THE CHILDREN TO—

WAIT! PLEASE, DAD. IF YOU DON'T KEEP YOUR STORY CHRONOLOGICAL, I'LL NEVER GET IT STRAIGHT ... TELL ME MORE ABOUT 1941 AND 1942.

SO?... OKAY. I'LL MAKE IT SO HOW YOU WANT IT. 1941?... AT THE END OF 1941 THE GERMANS CAME WITH SOMETHING NEW. WOLFE RAN FROM THE GEMEINDER ...

LOOK! THEY'RE PUTTING THESE UP ALL OVER TOWN.

ORDER

All Jews of Sosnowiec must be relocated into the Stara Sosnowiec quarter by January 1, 1942. Non-Jews will be moved into vacated premises.

Monek Merin

ALL 12 OF OUR HOUSEHOLD WERE GIVEN NOW TO LIVE IN 2½ SMALL ROOMS...

REWARD

FOR EVERY UNREGISTERED JEW YOU FIND: 1 KILO of SUGAR

MOST PEOPLE GOT EVEN *LESS* SPACE. BUT FATHER-IN-LAW AND WOLFE HAD A LITTLE *INFLUENCE*...

BUT THIS WASN'T YET A REAL GHETTO. STILL YOU COULD GO INTO OTHER PARTS OF TOWN SO LONG YOU WERE HOME AT NIGHT-TIME

HOLD THE LADDER, ANJA.

I'M PUTTING UP A CURTAIN TO GIVE US SOME PRIVACY.

TOSHA *INSISTED* ON GETTING THE PART OF THE ROOM WITH THE WINDOW.

IT DOESN'T MATTER, VLADEK. I'M JUST GLAD THE WHOLE FAMILY CAN STAY TOGETHER.

IT WAS NO MORE THE LUXURY LIFE WE HAD BEFORE.

FOR A COUPLE MONTHS I DID HERE STILL MY BLACK MARKET BUSINESS. THEN CAME MORE BAD NEWS, VERY BAD...

WHAT'S WRONG, FATHER?

THEY JUST ARRESTED MY FRIEND, NAHUM COHN, AND HIS SON.

THEY'VE TAKEN *FOUR* JEWS AWAY FOR DEALING GOODS WITHOUT COUPONS.

I DID MUCH BUSINESS WITH COHN!

THE GERMANS INTEND TO MAKE AN *EXAMPLE* OF THEM!

THE NEXT DAY I WALKED OVER TO MODRZEJOWSKA STREET AND I SAW THEM...

THEY HANGED THERE ONE FULL WEEK.

COHN HAD A DRY GOODS STORE. HE WAS KNOWN OVER ALL SOSNOWIEC. OFTEN HE GAVE ME CLOTH WITH NO COUPONS.

I TRADED ALSO WITH PFEFER, A FINE YOUNG MAN-A ZIONIST. HE WAS JUST MARRIED. HIS WIFE RAN SCREAMING IN THE STREET.

I WAS FRIGHTENED TO GO OUTSIDE FOR A FEW DAYS... I DIDN'T WANT TO PASS WHERE THEY WERE HANGING.

AND MAYBE ONE OF THEM COULD HAVE TALKED OF ME TO THE GERMANS TO TRY TO SAVE HIMSELF.

ACH. WHEN I THINK NOW OF THEM, IT **STILL** MAKES ME CRY... LOOK-EVEN FROM MY **DEAD** EYE TEARS ARE COMING OUT!

WHAT WAS ANJA DOING AT AROUND THIS TIME?

HOUSEWORKS... AND KNITTING... READING... AND SHE WAS WRITING ALWAYS HER DIARY.

I USED TO SEE POLISH NOTEBOOKS AROUND THE HOUSE AS A KID. WERE THOSE HER *DIARIES*?

YES, AND ALSO NO.

HER DIARIES DIDN'T SURVIVE FROM THE WAR. WHAT YOU SAW SHE WROTE AFTER: HER WHOLE STORY FROM THE START.

OHMIGOD! WHERE ARE THEY? I **NEED** THOSE FOR THIS BOOK!

COFF! PLEASE, ARTIE, STOP WITH THE SMOKING. IT MAKES ME SHORT WITH BREATH.

I THINK IT'S ALL YOUR PEDALING!

DON'T BE SO SMART! ...WHAT I WAS TELLING YOU? YES... AFTER THE HANGING I LOOKED FOR ANOTHER BUSINESS ...

...I STARTED TO TRADE GOLD AND JEWELRY.

IT WAS EASIER TO HIDE THAN CLOTHINGS. I KEPT THINGS HIDDEN IN THE CHILD'S STROLLER, AND I MADE A FEW ZLOTYS.

FOR A WHILE I HAD ALSO A FOOD BUSINESS THAT I DIDN'T YET TELL YOU....

I MET SZKLARCZYK. HE HAD A BIG GROCERY ON MODRZEJOWSKA..

YOU'RE ZYLBERBERG'S SON-IN-LAW, RIGHT? COME INSIDE AND WAIT FOR THE RAIN TO STOP.

SO, TOGETHER WE SAT AND SPOKE, AND HE HELPED, FROM TIME TO TIME, A CUSTOMER...

SORRY. YOU DON'T HAVE ENOUGH COUPONS TO BUY ½ KILO OF SUGAR.

STILL... SHE WENT OUT WITH ½ KILO. I SMELLED I COULD ARRANGE SOMETHING.

THEN A LITTLE MORE WE SPOKE AND HE MADE TO ME A PROPOSITION...

MAYBE YOU COULD SELL MY "EXTRA" ITEMS TO SMALL SHOPS IN THE AREA ...UNDER THE COUNTER.

IT WAS DANGEROUS TO CARRY THESE THINGS-BUT MAYBE I COULD BE LUCKY.

WHEN SOMEBODY IS HUNGRY HE LOOKS FOR BUSINESS....

ONE TIME I HAD 10 OR 15 KILOS SUGAR TO DELIVER...

HALT, JEW! WHAT ARE YOU CARRYING?

WHAT WAS I SUPPOSED TO SAY? FOR THIS I COULD REALLY HANG!

SUGAR.

...I'M TAKING IT OVER TO MY GROCERY STORE.

OH. YOU HAVE A SHOP?

I MADE SO THEY WOULD THINK IT WAS LEGAL.

I WENT TO THE BACK DOOR WHERE I HAD TO DELIVER...

OPEN UP, POLDEK!

..I'VE GOT OUR SUGAR.

?!

AND THEY LEFT ME GO WITHOUT EVEN CHECKING MY PAPERS!

85

BUT WHEN WE CAME TO STARA SOSNOWIEC, ALL MY BUSINESSES BECAME HARDER... IT WAS NOT SO EASY TO MOVE AROUND.

THE TIN SHOP FINISHED—THE OWNER WAS THE ONLY JEW THEY LET WORK THERE. I GOT THEN A JOB IN A GERMAN CARPENTRY SHOP.

FATHER-IN-LAW AND LOLEK WORKED ALREADY THERE, FOR REALLY NO MONEY. I DIDN'T NEED THIS BEFORE, BUT NOW I HAD TO HAVE THE WORK PAPER.

WOLFE COULD HAVE ARRANGED ME A JOB AT THE GEMEINDE... BUT I DIDN'T WANT TO PUT MY HANDS THERE WHERE JEWS WERE BEING TAKEN.

AND THEN IT CAME **AGAIN** SOMETHING NEW FROM THE GERMANS. WE GOT A NOTICE...

"ALL JEWS OVER 70 YEARS OLD WILL BE TRANSFERED TO THERESIENSTADT IN CZECHOSLOVAKIA ON MAY 10, 1942...

"...A COMMUNITY BETTER PREPARED TO TAKE CARE OF THE ELDERLY THAN OURS IN SOSNOWIEC..."

IT DOESN'T **LOOK** TOO BAD!

LIKE A CONVALESCENT HOME.

NOTICE:

ANJA'S GRANDPARENTS HAD ABOUT 90 YEARS.

WE'VE BEEN TOGETHER—A FAMILY—FOR 70 YEARS. WE DON'T WANT TO BREAK APART NOW!

DON'T WORRY. WE WON'T LET THEM TAKE YOU.

WE DIDN'T YET **KNOW** OF AUSCHWITZ—OF THE OVENS—BUT WE WERE **ANYWAY** AFRAID.

...SO, IN THE YARD, WE MADE A HIDING PLACE, A BUNKER...

CUT-AWAY VIEW:

WE SNEAKED FOOD TO THEM, AND—WHEN IT WAS SAFE—WE TOOK THEM INSIDE A LITTLE.

STORAGE SHEDS

FALSE WALL

GRANDPARENTS

SEVERAL TIMES CAME THE JEWISH POLICE TO OUR HOUSE...

OUR RECORDS SHOW THAT MR. AND MRS. KARMIO LIVE HERE. THEY HAVEN'T REGISTERED FOR TRANSFER.

YES - MY WIFE'S PARENTS - THEY LEFT WITHOUT A WORD A MONTH AGO.

JEWISH POLICE?

YES - WITH BIG STICKS.

SOME JEWS THOUGHT IN THIS WAY: IF THEY GAVE TO THE GERMANS A FEW JEWS, THEY COULD SAVE THE REST.

AND AT LEAST THEY COULD SAVE THEMSELVES.

AND A MONTH AFTER, THEY AGAIN CAME TO FATHER-IN-LAW.

MR. ZYLBERBERG, YOU AND YOUR WIFE MUST COME WITH US.

IF THE KARMIOS DON'T TURN UP IN 3 DAYS YOU TWO WILL BE SENT IN THEIR PLACE!

HE HAD STILL A LITTLE "PROTECTION" FROM THE GEMEIN-DE, SO THEY TOOK ONLY HIM AWAY - NOT HIS WIFE.

HE SAT A FEW DAYS THERE, THEN HE SENT TO US A NOTE

HE WROTE THAT WE HAD TO GIVE OVER THE GRANDPARENTS. EVEN IF THEY TOOK ONLY HIM AWAY NOW, NEXT THEY WOULD GRAB HIS WIFE, AND THEN THE REST OF THE FAMILY.

SO, WHAT HAPPENED?

WHAT HAPPENED? WE HAD TO DELIVER THEM!

THEY THOUGHT IT WAS TO THERESIENSTADT THEY WERE GOING.

LET US KNOW IF YOU NEED ANYTHING!

BUT THEY WENT RIGHT AWAY TO AUSCHWITZ, TO THE GAS.

WHEN DID YOU FIRST HEAR ABOUT AUSCHWITZ?

RIGHT AWAY WE HEARD...

EVEN FROM THERE - FROM THAT OTHER WORLD-PEOPLE CAME BACK AND TOLD US. BUT WE DIDN'T BELIEVE.

THEN THIS SAME NEWS CAME MORE AND MORE, SO WE BELIEVED. AND LATER ON, WE SAW ... EVEN WORSE!

AFTER WHAT HAPPENED TO THE GRANDPARENTS, IT WAS A FEW MONTHS QUIET. THEN IT CAME POSTERS EVERYWHERE AND SPEECHES FROM THE GEMEINDE...

FELLOW JEWS: ON WEDNESDAY, AUGUST 12TH, EVERY ONE OF YOU, YOUNG AND OLD, MALE AND FEMALE, HEALTHY AND SICK, MUST REGISTER AT THE DIENST STADIUM...

OH NO!

NOW WHAT?

...THERE'S NO CAUSE FOR ALARM - IT'S ONLY A MATTER OF INSPECTING YOUR DOCUMENTS AND STAMPING THEM. THIS WILL PROTECT YOU AS CITIZENS OF THE REGION!...

I'M NOT GOING. IT'S A NAZI TRAP!...

EVERYBODY WAS WORRIED.

...AND OUR JEWISH COMMITTEE IS HELPING THOSE MURDERERS. GOD KNOWS WHAT WILL HAPPEN TO US AT THE STADIUM!

WELL, THEY JUST INSPECTED JEWISH DOCUMENTS IN SOME NEARBY TOWNS. IT WAS NO BIG DEAL.

ANYWAY, WE'VE GOT TO GO. WITHOUT LEGAL PAPERS, WE'RE LOST!

TO GO, IT WAS NO GOOD. BUT, NOT TO GO - IT WAS ALSO NO GOOD.

MY FATHER- HE HAD 62 YEARS -CAME BY STREETCAR TO ME FROM DABROWA, THE VILLAGE NEXT DOOR FROM SOSNOWIEC.

AFTER MY MOTHER DIED WITH CANCER, HE LIVED THERE IN THE HOUSE OF MY SISTER FELA, AND HER FOUR SMALL CHILDREN.

HERE'S A COOKIE, RICHIEU. AUNT FELA BAKED IT FOR YOU.

SAY THANK YOU TO GRANDPA.

I NEED YOUR ADVICE, VLADEK. SHOULD I GO TO THE STADIUM ON WEDNESDAY, OR HIDE AT HOME?

I DON'T KNOW. I'M NOT EVEN SURE WHAT WE'RE GOING TO DO. ...ANJA'S MOTHER SAYS SHE ISN'T GO- ING. SHE'S SICK AND AFRAID.

AT LEAST ANJA'S FATHER, LOLEK AND I ALL WORK AT THE GERMAN WOODSHOP. WE'RE A LITTLE SAFER. BUT YOU DON'T WORK. YOU HAVE NO PAPERS. YOU DON'T HAVE ANYTHING!

WELL, OUR COUSIN MORDECAI SAYS HE'LL BE AT ONE OF THE INSPECTION TABLES. I COULD BRING MY PAPERS TO HIM...

WHAT DOES FELA SAY?

SHE'S NOT SURE...BUT IF FELA DECIDES TO GO, OF COURSE I'LL GO WITH HER.

CAN I HAVE ANOTHER COOKIE?

RICHIEU!

REALLY, I DIDN'T KNOW HOW TO ADVISE HIM.

BUT FINALLY HE DID GO. PEOPLE WERE AFRAID TO NOT SHOW UP.

SO IT CAME TO THE STADIUM ALMOST ALL THE JEWS OF SOSNOWIEC, AND FROM THE OTHER VILLAGES NEAR, MAYBE 25 OR 30,000 PEOPLE.

EVERYONE CAME VERY NICE DRESSED. THEY TRIED SO THAT THEY WOULD LOOK YOUNG AND ABLE TO WORK, IN ORDER TO GET A GOOD STAMP ON THEIR PASSPORT.

WHEN WE WERE EVERYBODY INSIDE, GESTAPO WITH MACHINE GUNS SURROUNDED THE STADIUM.

LINE UP BY FAMILY AT THE TABLES TO REGISTER! QUICKLY!

THEN WAS A SELECTION, WITH PEOPLE SENT EITHER TO THE LEFT, EITHER TO THE RIGHT.

OLD PEOPLE, FAMILIES WITH LOTS OF KIDS, AND PEOPLE WITHOUT WORK CARDS ARE ALL GOING TO THE LEFT!

WE UNDERSTOOD THIS MUST BE VERY BAD.

ME AND ANJA CAME TO THE TABLE WHERE MY COUSIN WAS SITTING...

AH, YOU WORK AT THE CARPENTRY SHOP... GO TO THE RIGHT.

SO WE GOT STAMPED OUR PASSPORTS AND CAME QUICK TO THE GOOD SIDE OF THE STADIUM. THOSE THEY SENT LEFT, THEY DIDN'T GET ANY STAMP.

90

WE WERE SO HAPPY WE CAME THROUGH. BUT WE WORRIED NOW—WERE OUR FAMILIES SAFE?

LOOK! THERE'S POPPA, WITH LOLEK AND LONIA!

WE SAW WOLFE AND TOSHA. OUR FAMILY SEEMS TO BE OKAY.

DID YOU SEE MY FATHER?

I COULDN'T SEE ANYWHERE MY FATHER.

BUT LATER SOMEONE WHO SAW HIM TOLD ME... HE CAME THROUGH THIS SAME COUSIN OVER TO THE GOOD SIDE.

HER, THEY SENT TO THE LEFT. FOUR CHILDREN WAS TOO MANY.

SPIEGELMAN... TO THE RIGHT.

THEN CAME FELA TO REGISTER...

FELA!

MY DAUGHTER! HOW CAN SHE MANAGE ALONE—WITH FOUR CHILDREN TO TAKE CARE OF?

AND, WHAT DO YOU THINK? HE SNEAKED ON TO THE BAD SIDE!

AND THOSE ON THE BAD SIDE NEVER CAME ANYMORE HOME.

THOSE WITH A STAMP WERE LET TO GO HOME. BUT THERE WERE VERY FEW JEWS NOW LEFT IN SOSNOWIEC...

ONE FROM THREE THEY KEPT AT THE STADIUM.... MAYBE 10,000 PEOPLE—AND WITH THEM, MY FATHER.

WELL....IT'S ENOUGH FOR TODAY. YES, ARTIE?...

WHOO—I OVERDID A LITTLE. I'M FEELING DIZZY.

MAYBE YOU SHOULD LIE DOWN A WHILE.

ARE YOU FINISHED?

UH-HUH. MY FATHER'S WORN OUT. HE'S TAKING A NAP.

HE WAS JUST TELLING ME ABOUT THE TIME EVERYONE IN SOSNOWIEC HAD TO GET HIS PASSPORT STAMPED.

IN THE STADIUM? YES... THEY GOT MY MOTHER THEN.

SHE WAS TAKEN, WITH EVERYBODY ELSE WHO WAS GOING TO BE DEPORTED, TO FOUR APARTMENT HOUSES THAT WERE EMPTIED TO MAKE A SORT OF PRISON...

THEY PUT THOUSANDS OF PEOPLE THERE... IT WAS SO CROWDED THAT SOME OF THEM ACTUALLY SUFFOCATED... NO FOOD... NO TOILETS. IT WAS *TERRIBLE*.

PEOPLE JUMPED OUT THE WINDOWS TO END THEIR MISERY A LITTLE QUICKER.

GOD.

BUT MY MOTHER *SURVIVED* THAT. HER BROTHER WAS ON THE JEWISH COMMITTEE, AND HE HID HER IN A COAL CELLAR 'TIL ALL THE TRANSPORTS LEFT.

THEN HE GOT ME A JOB SCRUBBING THE PEOPLE'S FILTH—VOMIT! EXCREMENT!— OUT OF SEVERAL APARTMENTS, AND I MANAGED TO SMUGGLE HER OUT.

EVENTUALLY SHE AND MY FATHER BOTH ENDED UP IN AUSCHWITZ. THEY DIED THERE.

WHERE ARE YOU GOING? YOU DIDN'T DRINK YOUR COFFEE.

I JUST THOUGHT OF SOMETHING. MY FATHER MENTIONED THAT ANJA USED TO KEEP A DIARY, AND I *VAGUELY* REMEMBER SEEING THEM ON HIS SHELVES IN THE DEN.

I DOUBT IT. I WOULD HAVE NOTICED THEM.

WELL, THERE'S SO MUCH JUNK IN THERE, IT'S WORTH A SHOT.

LOOK AT ALL THIS STUFF!...OLD MENUS HE PICKED UP ON CRUISES. ...A PILE OF STATIONERY FROM THE PINES HOTEL...

INCREDIBLE! FOUR 1965 DRY DOCK SAVINGS BANK CALENDARS...I'LL BET HE NEVER EVEN HAD AN ACCOUNT THERE.

HE DRIVES ME CRAZY! HE WON'T EVEN LET ME THROW OUT THE PLASTIC PITCHER HE TOOK FROM HIS HOSPITAL ROOM LAST YEAR!

HE'S MORE ATTACHED TO THINGS THAN TO PEOPLE!

I REALLY DON'T KNOW HOW LONG I CAN TAKE HIM. I REALLY DON'T.

I BETTER BE GETTING HOME. I'LL LOOK FOR THOSE DIARIES NEXT TIME.

WAIT! PUT EVERYTHING BACK EXACTLY LIKE IT WAS, OR I'LL NEVER HEAR THE END OF IT!

OKAY... OKAY... RELAX.

93

MNF?

HELLO, ARTIE? I'M TELLING YOU, I DON'T KNOW WHAT TO DO WITH YOUR FATHER—HE JUST CLIMBED ONTO THE ROOF!..

UNH? MALA?

HE INSISTED ON FIXING THE DRAINPIPE AND GOT DIZZY! I DON'T KNOW HOW I EVER GOT HIM DOWN!

WHAT TIME IS IT?

NOW HE WANTS TO CLIMB BACK UP! WHAT AM I SUPPOSED TO DO?!

PLEASE DON'T SHOUT.

WHY DON'T YOU CALL A HANDYMAN? JEEZ, MALA, IT'S ONLY 7:30 AM. FRANÇOISE AND I WERE UP 'TIL 4:00! YOU KNOW WE DON'T GET UP 'TIL—

HELLO? ARTIE? IT'S POPPA HERE.

I'M TELLING YOU, MALA MAKES ME MESHUGAH! I WANT THAT MAYBE YOU COULD COME NOW TO QUEENS TO HELP ME.

WHAT? YOU'VE GOTTA BE KIDDING!

WHEN I WAS YOUNG I COULD DO BY MYSELF THESE THINGS. BUT NOW, DARLING, I NEED IT YOUR HELP FOR THE DRAINPIPE!

UM—LOOK, POP. I'LL CALL YOU BACK AFTER I'VE HAD SOME COFFEE.

WHEW. MAYBE I WAS DREAMING.

WUZZIT? YOUR FATHER AGAIN?

UH-HUH. HE WANTS ME TO GO HELP HIM FIX HIS ROOF OR SOMETHING. *SHIT!* EVEN AS A KID I HATED HELPING HIM AROUND THE HOUSE.

HE LOVED SHOWING OFF HOW *HANDY* HE WAS... AND PROVING THAT ANYTHING *I* DID WAS ALL WRONG.

HE MADE ME COMPLETELY NEUROTIC ABOUT FIXING STUFF.

I MEAN, I DIDN'T EVEN OWN A *HAMMER* BEFORE WE MOVED INTO THIS PLACE!

ONE REASON I BECAME AN ARTIST WAS THAT HE THOUGHT IT WAS IMPRACTICAL—JUST A WASTE OF TIME...

...IT WAS AN AREA WHERE I WOULDN'T HAVE TO COMPETE WITH HIM.

SO... ARE YOU GOING OUT TO QUEENS?

NO WAY—I'D RATHER FEEL GUILTY! BESIDES, I'M TOO BUSY, AND HE CAN EASILY AFFORD TO HIRE SOMEBODY.

UH, HELLO POP. LISTEN... ABOUT THAT DRAINPIPE... I DON'T THINK I CAN COME. I—

SO? NEVER MIND ARTIE...

I TALKED JUST NOW TO FRANK, WHAT LIVES NEXT DOOR. HE AGREED HE WOULD FIX WITH ME OVER THE WEEKEND.

THAT'S GREAT!

YES. OF COURSE, BETTER IT WOULD BE FIXED TODAY—BUT AT LEAST *SOMEBODY* WILL HELP ME!

JUST GREAT.

About a week later, early afternoon...

HI, MALA.

OY! YOU SCARED ME, ARTIE. MY NERVES ARE COMPLETELY SHOT, LIVING WITH YOUR FATHER.

HE SEEMED A LITTLE UPSET WHEN I SAW HIM DOWNSTAIRS... DO YOU THINK HE'S ANGRY THAT I DIDN'T COME HELP HIM LAST WEEK?

I DON'T THINK SO...

BUT KEEPING THIS HOUSE FIXED UP IS TOO MUCH FOR HIM NOW. I KEEP TELLING HIM TO SELL IT AND BUY A CONDO IN MIAMI.

HE SEEMS DEPRESSED.

IT COULD BE THAT COMIC STRIP YOU ONCE MADE — THE ONE ABOUT YOUR MOTHER.

WHAT?

VLADEK SAW IT FOR THE FIRST TIME A COUPLE OF DAYS AGO.

HOW DO YOU KNOW ABOUT "PRISONER ON THE HELL PLANET"?

MY FRIEND, RUTHIE, HAS A SON IN COLLEGE. HE READS ALL THE COMICS. HE SHOWED IT TO HER, AND SHE GAVE ME A COPY.

SHIT!...

I KNEW IT WOULD UPSET YOUR FATHER, SO I KEPT IT HIDDEN. BUT, SOMEHOW HE FOUND IT.

I DREW THIS STORY YEARS AGO.

IT APPEARED IN AN OBSCURE UNDERGROUND COMIC BOOK. I NEVER THOUGHT VLADEK WOULD SEE IT.

PRISONER ON THE HELL PLANET

PRISONER ON THE HELL PLANET
A CASE HISTORY

TROJAN LAKE, N.Y. 1958

IN 1968 MY MOTHER KILLED HERSELF. SHE LEFT NO NOTE!

MY FATHER FOUND HER IN THE BATHTUB WHEN HE GOT HOME FROM WORK... HER WRISTS SLASHED AND AN EMPTY BOTTLE OF PILLS NEAR-BYE ....

I WAS LIVING WITH MY PARENTS FOR THE MOST PART (AS I AGREED TO DO ON MY RELEASE FROM THE STATE MENTAL HOSPITAL SEVERAL MONTHS BEFORE).

I HAD JUST SPENT THE WEEK-END WITH MY GIRLFRIEND, (MY PARENTS DIDN'T LIKE HER) I WAS LATE GETTING HOME .....

OY, GOTT!

SUBWAY

RECORDS

I SUPPOSE THAT IF I'D GOTTEN HOME WHEN EXPECTED, I WOULD HAVE FOUND HER BODY ....

63-12

WHEN I SAW THE CROWD I HAD A PANG OF FEAR... I SUSPECTED THE WORST, BUT I DIDN'T LET MYSELF KNOW!

A COUSIN HERDED ME AWAY FROM THE SCENE:

COME TO THE DOCTOR'S.... YOUR MOTHER IS -AH- SICK!... HE WILL EXPLAIN ......

DOCTOR ORENS LIVED NEARBYE......

SIT DOWN, ARTHUR... I THOUGHT I SHOULD BE THE ONE TO TELL YOU...

YOUR MOTHER KILLED HERSELF — SHE'S DEAD!

I COULD AVOID THE TRUTH NO LONGER—THE DOCTOR'S WORDS CLATTERED INSIDE ME.... I FELT CONFUSED; I FELT ANGRY; I FELT NUMB!... I DIDN'T EXACTLY FEEL LIKE CRYING, BUT FIGURED I SHOULD!....

SHE'S DEAD! A SUICIDE!

NOW, NOW BOY...

NO, LET HIM CRY— IT'S GOOD FOR HIM!

WE WENT HOME... MY FATHER HAD COMPLETELY FALLEN APART!....

OY, ARTIE! WHY? WHY! SUCH A TRAGEDY! AND NOT EVEN A NOTE!!!

I WAS EXPECTED TO COMFORT HIM!

MOTHER... MOTHER...,

SOMEHOW THE FUNERAL ARRANGEMENTS WERE MADE...

...AND FOR $950⁰⁰ WE HAVE A BRONZE CASKET WITH BRONZE COLORED VELVET— OF COURSE, FOR $2,000⁰⁰ WE CAN...

PROTECT WHAT YOU HAVE

THAT NIGHT WAS BAD...
MY FATHER INSISTED WE
SLEEP ON THE FLOOR—AN OLD
JEWISH CUSTOM, I GUESS.
HE HELD ME AND MOANED
TO HIMSELF ALL NIGHT.
I WAS UNCOMFORTABLE...
WE WERE SCARED!

THE NEXT DAY AT THE FUNERAL HOME WAS WORSE...

MY FATHER FOUGHT FOR SELF-CONTROL AND PRAYED
I WAS PRETTY *SPACED OUT* IN THOSE DAYS—I RECI
TO MY MOTHER FROM *THE TIBETAN BOOK OF THE DEA*

"O NOBLY BORN... IN YOUR
JOURNEY THROUGH THE FOR
LESS VOID, REMEMBER TH
UNITY OF ALL LIVING THINGS

IT WAS TOO MUCH—I HAD TO LEAVE...

A FRIEND OF THE FAMILY FOUND ME OUT IN THE HALL....

NOW YOU CRY!
BETTER YOU CRIED
WHEN YOUR MOTHER
WAS STILL ALIVE!

I FELT NAUSEOUS .... THE GUILT WAS OVERWHELMING!

THE NEXT WEEK WE SPENT IN MOURNING... MY FATHER'S FRIENDS ALL OFFERED ME HOSTILITY MIXED IN WITH THEIR CONDO-LENCES....

ARTHUR—WE'RE SO SORRY...

IT'S HIS FAULT— THE PUNK!

THEY THINK IT'S MY FAULT!!

...BUT, FOR THE MOST PART, I WAS LEFT ALONE WITH MY THOUGHTS...

MENOPAUSAL DEPRESSION

HITLER DID IT!

MOMMY!

BITCH

...I REMEMBERED THE LAST TIME I SAW HER...

...ARTIE...

SHE CAME INTO MY ROOM... IT WAS LATE AT NIGHT....

...ARTIE ... YOU ... STILL ... LOVE ... ME ...., DON'T YOU?....

...I TURNED AWAY, RESENTFUL OF THE WAY SHE TIGHTENED THE UMBILICAL CORD...

SURE, MA!

...SHE WALKED OUT AND CLOSED THE DOOR!

CLIK!

AGH!

WELL, MOM, IF YOU'RE LISTENING...

CONGRATULATIONS!... YOU'VE COMMITTED THE PERFECT CRIME ....

...YOU PUT ME HERE .... SHORTED ALL MY CIR-CUITS...CUT MY NERVE ENDINGS ...AND CROSSED MY WIRES!....

...YOU MURDERED ME, MOMMY, AND YOU LEFT ME HERE TO TAKE THE RAP!!!

PIPE DOWN, MAC! SOME OF US ARE TRYING TO SLEEP!

© art spiegelman, 1972

GEE, I'M SURPRISED THAT VLADEK *READ* THIS WHEN HE FOUND IT. HE *NEVER* READS COMICS...

HE DOESN'T EVEN LOOK AT MY WORK WHEN I STICK IT UNDER HIS NOSE.

BUT THIS ISN'T *LIKE* OTHER COMICS...

I TELL YOU, WHEN RUTHIE SHOWED IT TO ME I THOUGHT I'D *FAINT*, I WAS SO SHOCKED.

IT WAS SO... SO *PERSONAL!*

...BUT VERY ACCURATE... OBJECTIVE. I SPENT A LOT OF TIME HELPING OUT HERE AFTER ANJA'S FUNERAL. IT WAS JUST AS YOU SAID.

SO, ARTIE. I'M READY.

LET'S WALK NOW TO THE BANK TOGETHER.

MALA JUST TOLD ME THAT YOU SAW MY COMIC... THE ONE ABOUT MOM.

YES. I FOUND IT WHEN I LOOKED FOR THE THINGS YOU ASKED ME LAST TIME. *HOO!* I SAW THE PICTURE THERE OF MOM, SO I READ IT... AND I CRIED.

I-I'M SORRY.

IT'S GOOD YOU GOT IT OUTSIDE YOUR SYSTEM. BUT FOR ME IT BROUGHT IN MY MIND SO MUCH *MEMORIES* OF ANJA.

...OF COURSE I'M THINKING ALWAYS ABOUT HER *ANYWAY.*

YES. YOU KEEP PHOTOS OF HER ALL AROUND YOUR DESK—LIKE A SHRINE!

WHAT HAVE I TO DO, MALA? IN THE GARBAGE PUT THEM? OF YOU *ALSO* I HAVE A PHOTO ON THE DESK!

ACH! DON'T DO ME ANY FAVORS!

YOU SEE WHAT I HAVE WITH HER? ALWAYS, WHATEVER I DO IS NO GOOD.

DID YOU FIND MOM'S DIARY?

SO FAR THIS DIDN'T SHOW UP. I LOOKED, BUT I CAN'T FIND.

I'VE **GOT** TO HAVE THAT!

ANOTHER TIME I'LL AGAIN LOOK. BUT NOW BETTER WE GO TO THE BANK.

OKAY.

..EVERY DAY I WALK, OTHERWISE IN MY LEGS THE CIRCULATION MAKES ME A CRAMP- IT'S SOMETHING TERRIBLE AND I CAN'T SLEEP.

BUT FOR MY HEART, I MUST WALK SLOW.

WHAT HAPPENED TO YOU AND ANJA AFTER THE BIG SELECTION AT THE STADIUM?

WELL, FOR A TIME IT WAS EVERYTHING QUIET. THEN IN 1943 CAME AN ORDER: ALL JEWS WHAT ARE LEFT IN SOSNOWIEC MUST GO TO LIVE IN AN OLD VILLAGE NEARBY CALLED SRODULA.

AND THE POLES OF SRODULA, WE JEWS HAD TO PAY TO MOVE THEM TO **OUR** HOUSES IN SOSNOWIEC... AND HERE IN SRODULA WOULD BE OUR GHETTO TO LIVE EVER AFTER.

WOHNGEBIE
JUDEN
BETRETE

OUR FAMILY GOT A COTTAGE-LESS SPACE THAN BEFORE, BUT WE HAD AT LEAST WHERE TO LIVE. MANY LIVED ONLY IN THE STREET.

...YOU'VE ALL HEARD THE STORIES ABOUT AUSCHWITZ. HORRIBLE UNBELIEVABLE STORIES.

THEY CAN'T BE TRUE!

ONE THING IS CERTAIN— AS BAD AS THINGS ARE IN THE GHETTO, BEING DE-PORTED IS EVEN WORSE.

PLEASE! IT'S BAD LUCK TO EVEN SPEAK OF IT!

LOOK, YOU DON'T HAVE MUCH INFLUENCE HERE. IN ZAWIERCIE I HAVE SOME INFLUENCE WITH THE GERMANS ... I CAN BRIBE THEM.

MY 90-YEAR-OLD FATHER STILL LIVES WITH ME...WHENEVER THERE'S A ROUND-UP, AN S.S. MAN GUARDS HIM TO KEEP HIM SAFE!

NINETY! THIS WAS 1943! IT WASN'T **LEFT** ANY OTHER JEWS WHAT HAD NINETY YEARS!

PERSIS WAS REALLY A FINE MAN—NOT SO LIKE MONIEK MERIN, THE HEAD OF **OUR** GHETTO, WHO LOOKED ONLY OUT FOR HIMSELF. ...PERSIS TRIED REALLY TO HELP HIS JEWS.

I CAN MANAGE PAPERS TO TAKE WOLFE, TOSHA AND BIBI—AND MAYBE LITTLE LONIA AND RICHIEU IF YOU'LL LET ME.

YES. THEY'D BE BETTER OFF.

YOU SEE? I WANTED TO SEND RICHIEU SOMEPLACE SAFE A **YEAR** AGO— WITH ILZECKI'S CHILD!

THINGS ARE EVEN WORSE NOW, VLADEK. WE HAVE NO CHOICE!

NO! WE MUST ALL STAY TOGETHER! WE'VE MADE IT THIS FAR. GOD WILL STILL HELP US!

MATKA! BE REALISTIC!

ANJA'S MOTHER DIDN'T LIKE TO LOOK AT THE FACTS. BUT FINALLY EVEN SHE AGREED,

SO PERSIS ARRANGED, AND HE CAME AGAIN TO SRODULA.

IT WENT WITH HIM WOLFE, TOSHA AND BIBI

LOLEK'S LITTLE SISTER, LONIA

AND OUR BOY, RICHIEU.

WE WATCHED UNTIL THEY DISAPPEARED FROM OUR EYES...

IT WAS THE LAST TIME EVER WE SAW THEM; BUT THAT WE COULDN'T KNOW.

WHEN THINGS CAME WORSE IN OUR GHETTO WE SAID ALWAYS: "THANK GOD THE KIDS ARE WITH PERSIS, SAFE

THAT SPRING, ON ONE DAY, THE GERMANS TOOK FROM SRODULA TO AUSCHWITZ OVER 1,000 PEOPLE.

MOST THEY TOOK WERE KIDS — SOME ONLY 2 OR 3 YEARS.

SOME KIDS WERE SCREAMING AND SCREAMING. THEY COULDN'T STOP.

SO THE GERMANS SWINGED THEM BY THE LEGS AGAINST A WALL...

AND THEY NEVER ANYMORE SCREAMED.

IN THIS WAY THE GERMANS TREATED THE LITT ONES WHAT STILL HAD SURVIVED A LITTLE.

THIS I DIDN'T SEE WITH M OWN EYES, BUT SOMEBOD THE NEXT DAY TOLD ME AND I SAID, "THANK GOD WITH PERSIS OUR CHILDREN ARE SAFE!"

SO..WHAT HAPPENED TO RICHIEU?

ACH! OUR BEAUTIFUL BOY. WE ONLY FOUND OUT MUCH LATER.

A FEW MONTHS AFTER WE SENT RICHIEU TO ZAWIERCIE, THE GERMANS DECIDED THEY WOULD FINISH OUT THAT GHETTO.

BANG BANG

MORE GUNSHOTS! WHAT'S GOING ON?

IT'S HORRIBLE, TOSHA!...

ALL THE GESTAPO IN THE GHETTO HAVE BEEN REPLACED BY OTHERS FROM OPOLE. THEY JUST SHOT PERSIS AND THE REST OF THE JEWISH COUNCIL!..

WHAT?

THEY'RE EVACUATING ZAWIERCIE. WE'RE ALL SUPPOSED TO GO TO THE SQUARE WITH OUR BAGGAGE RIGHT AWAY. THEY'RE SENDING ALL OF US OUT— TO AUSCHWITZ!

OH MY GOD.

NO!

I WON'T GO TO THEIR GAS CHAMBERS!...

AND MY **CHILDREN** WON'T GO TO THEIR GAS CHAMBERS.

BIBI! LONIA! RICHIEU! COME HERE QUICKLY!

ALWAYS TOSHA CARRIED AROUND HER NECK SOME POISON...SHE KILLED NOT ONLY HERSELF, BUT ALSO THE 3 CHILDREN.

I'M TELLING YOU, IT WAS A TRAGEDY AMONG TRAGEDIES. HE WAS SUCH A HAPPY, BEAUTIFUL BOY!

THEN, IN JUNE, THEY ARRESTED MONIEK MERIN AND ALL THE OTHER HIGHEST BIG SHOTS OF THE *JUDENRAT*, THE JEWISH COUNCIL.

false wall
BUNKER
ATTIC
Entrance hidden by chandelie...
UPSTAIRS BEDROOM

AROUND THIS TIME WE WERE PUT INTO A DIFFERENT HOUSE. HERE ALSO WE MADE A BUNKER.

BY THE END OF JULY THE NAZIS MADE TO LIQUIDATE COMPLETELY OUR GHETTO - IT WAS 10,000 JEWS TAKEN AWAY IN ONE WEEK.

EXCEPT TO SNEAK FOR FOOD, WE STAYED MOSTLY IN THE BUNKER.

LOLEK! THANK GOD YOU'RE SAFE!

IT'S LIKE A BATTLEFIELD OUTSIDE!

THERE'S HARDLY ANYONE LEFT IN SRODULA. EVERYONE HAS BEEN DEPORTED OR SHOT.

FROM ALL THE JEWS OF ALL SOSNOWIEC IT WAS LEFT MAYBE 1,000 IN THE GHETTO.

AT LEAST YOUR BAG IS FULL... YOU FOUND A LOT OF FOOD, YES?

JUST A FEW OLD TURNIPS.... AND SOME BOOKS.

BOOKS!? WHAT'S THE MATTER WITH YOU? WE CAN'T EAT BOOKS!

SHH

ALL THE TIME WE WERE HUNGRY. WE JUST DIDN'T HAVE WHAT TO EAT.

ONE NIGHT WE WENT TO SNEAK FOR FOOD…

WE DRAGGED HIM UP TO OUR BUNKER

IN THE MORNING WE GAVE A LITTLE FOOD TO HIM AND LEFT HIM GO TO HIS FAMILY…

WE WERE MAYBE 200 PEOPLE TOGETHER WAITING... EACH WEDNESDAY WENT VANS TO AUSCHWITZ. WHEN WE WERE CAUGHT, IT WAS THEN MAYBE A THURSDAY.

LOOK, ANJA! THAT'S MY COUSIN, JAKOV SPIEGELMAN, IN THE COURTYARD.

HEY! JAKOV! HELP! JAKOV-HELP US!

VLADEK?! THERE'S NOTHING I CAN DO!

I MADE SIGNS TO SHOW I COULD PAY.

SOME GOLD I HID IN THE CHIMNEY OF OUR BUNKER WHEN THEY TOOK US. BUT A FEW VALUABLES I HAD STILL WITH ME.

OKAY, DON'T WORRY! HASKEL WILL COME HELP YOU!

HASKEL SPIEGELMAN WAS ANOTHER COUSIN.

WOULDN'T THEY HAVE HELPED YOU EVEN IF YOU COULDN'T PAY? I MEAN, YOU WERE FROM THE SAME FAMILY..

HAH! YOU DON'T UNDERSTAND...

AT THAT TIME IT WASN'T ANYMORE FAMILIES. IT WAS EVERYBODY TO TAKE CARE FOR HIMSELF!

THE NEXT DAY CAME IN TWO GIRLS CARRYING FOOD. WITH THEM CAME HASKEL, A CHIEF OF THE JEWISH POLICE.

(LOOK, VLADEK. I CAN GET YOU AND YOUR WIFE OUT-EVEN YOUR NEPHEW. BUT YOUR IN-LAWS ARE TOO OLD. THEY'LL NEVER GET PAST THE GUARDS.)

PLEASE! WE'LL MAKE IT WORTH YOUR WHILE.

THE TWO GIRLS HE SENT BACK TO THE KITCHEN.

QUICK, BOY. GRAB THIS EMPTY PAIL AND CARRY IT OUT WITH ME.

FROM THE WINDOW WE SAW LOLEK GO.

MY GOD, VLADEK...

YOU **MUST** GET MATKA AND ME OUT TOO. GIVE YOUR COUSIN THIS GOLD WATCH, THIS DIAMOND-**ANYTHING!**

OF COURSE I-I'LL DO EVERY-THING I CAN.

THE DAY AFTER, ANJA AND I CARRIED PAST THE GUARDS THE EMPTY PAILS.

HASKEL TOOK FROM ME FATHER-IN-LAW'S JEWELS. BUT, FINALLY, HE *DIDN'T* HELP THEM.

ON WEDNESDAY THE VANS CAME. ANJA AND I SAW HER FATHER AT THE WINDOW. HE WAS TEARING HIS HAIR AND CRYING.

HE WAS A MILLIONAIRE, BUT EVEN THIS DIDN'T SAVE HIM HIS LIFE.

SO MOM'S PARENTS DIED IN AUSCHWITZ?

NU? WHAT ELSE? RIGHT AWAY THEY WENT TO THE GAS.

HASKEL WAS HAPPY TO TAKE FROM FATHER-IN-LAW THE JEWELS—BUT THE RISK TO SAVE THEM, THIS HE WAS **NOT** SO HAPPY TO TAKE.

ALWAYS HASKEL WAS SUCH A GUY: A *KOMBINATOR*.

A WHAT?

A GUY WHAT MAKES *KOMBINACYA*, A SCHEMER...A CROOK.

WHAT DID YOU PICK UP?

TELEPHONE WIRE. THIS IT'S VERY HARD TO FIND.

INSIDE IT'S **LITTLE** WIRES. IT'S GOOD FOR TYING THINGS.

YOU **ALWAYS** PICK UP TRASH! CAN'T YOU JUST BUY WIRE?

PSSH. WHY ALWAYS YOU WANT TO BUY WHEN YOU CAN **FIND**!? ANYWAY, THIS WIRE THEY DON'T HAVE IT IN ANY STORES.

I'LL GIVE TO YOU SOME WIRE. YOU'LL SEE HOW USEFUL IT IS.

NO THANKS! JUST TELL ME WHAT HAPPENED WITH HASKEL.

THERE ARE ONLY ABOUT A THOUSAND JEWS LEFT HERE. MOST WORK AT THE BRAUN SHOE SHOP.

HASKEL WAS A VERY BIG MAN IN THE GHETTO THEN, WHEN SRODULA WAS FINISHING.

I'LL REGISTER YOU BOTH THERE, AND – GOOD AFTERNOON, SERGEANT!

HOW ARE YOU, HERR SPIEGELMAN?

HASKEL PLAYED VERY OFTEN, CARDS WITH THE GESTAPO.

WE'LL SEE YOU TONIGHT, YES?

NATURALLY. I JUST HOPE YOU WON'T BE AS LUCKY AS LAST TIME.

HE LOST TO THEM BIG AMOUNTS OF MONEY, SO THEY WOULD LIKE HIM.

116

MILOCH-TAKE CARE OF COUSIN VLADEK.

GLADLY

BEN HERE CAN SHOW YOU HOW TO RESOLE THE GERMAN BOOTS.

HASKEL HAD 2 BROTHERS, PESACH AND MILOCH. PESACH WAS ALSO A *KOMBINATOR*. BUT MILOCH, HE WAS A FINE FELLOW.

WE'LL RESERVE THIS WORKBENCH FOR YOU...

YOU DON'T HAVE TO SIT HERE ALL THE TIME, BUT WHENEVER THE GERMAN COMMISSION COMES TO INSPECT, JUST SIT THERE AND LOOK BUSY...

FROM TIME TO TIME I HAD OTHER JOBS ALSO TO DO AROUND THE GHETTO...

YES! THIS REMINDS ME SOMETHING NOW...

REMEMBER THIS GUY WHAT I TOLD YOU GAVE US OUT OF OUR BUNKER?...

WELL, YOU KNOW, I BURIED HIM...

HEY! THIS IS THE RAT THAT TURNED MY FAMILY OVER TO THE GESTAPO.

HE WAS SHOT!

HASKEL HAD ARRANGED HE WOULD BE KILLED.

BUT IF HE'S DEAD WHY ARE HIS EYES STILL WIDE OPEN?

HE WAS STRUGGLING TO SURVIVE.

IT HAPPENED I WAS ON THE WORK DETAIL, SO... I BURIED HIM.

117

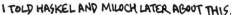
I TOLD HASKEL AND MILOCH LATER ABOUT THIS.

YOU WERE VERY LUCKY, VLADEK...

THEY CALL HIM "THE SHOOTER". EVERY DAY HE KILLS SOME POOR JEW, JUST FOR FUN.

HEY! AREN'T YOU GOING OVER TO PESACH'S TO BUY SOME CAKE?

CAKE?

FOR YEARS WE DIDN'T SEE ANY CAKE. HARDLY EVEN **BREAD** WE SAW!

BUT COUSIN PESACH WAS REALLY SELLING **CAKE!** EVERYONE WHAT COULD AFFORD IT STOOD ON LINE TO BUY A PIECE...

IT'S IM-POSSIBLE!

HE'S JOKING!

CAKE!

IT LOOKS DELICIOUS.

HOW DID YOU MAN-AGE IT, PESACH?

WHEN PEOPLE ARE SENT TO AUSCHWITZ, MY MEN SEARCH THEIR HOUSES.

PESACH WAS LIKE HASKEL, PART OF THE JEWISH POLICE.

THEY FIND A LITTLE FLOUR HERE, A FEW GRAMS OF SUGAR THERE...I SAVED IT!

HE WAS YOUNGER FROM HAS-KEL, BUT ALSO A "KOMBINATOR."

YOU KNOW WHAT A COOK MY RIFKA IS... TRY IT! ONLY 75 ZLOTYS A SLICE.

I HAD STILL SAVINGS, SO I GOT FOR ANJA AND ME SOME CAKE.

BUT, THE WHOLE GHETTO, WE WERE SO SICK LATER, YOU CAN'T IMAGINE ...

SOME OF THE FLOUR PESACH FOUND—IT WASN'T *REALLY* FLOUR, ONLY **LAUNDRY SOAP**, WHAT HE PUT IN THE CAKE BY MISTAKE.

OW! *

GROAN

OY!

OUCH!

...WE WERE, ALL OF US, SICK LIKE DOGS.

BEFORE THE WAR PESACH HAD A RESORT HOTEL IN ZAKOPANE...

IN THOSE DAYS ALSO HE FOUND ALWAYS SCHEMES.

ALL GUESTS HAD TO PAY BIG POLISH TAXES... SO PESACH TOOK BRIBES TO NOT REGISTER THEM. BUT IF AN INSPECTOR CAME, THE GUESTS HAD TO HIDE THEMSELVES AWAY.

ONE TIME HIS WIFE MADE NOT ENOUGH DESSERTS TO GIVE TO EVERYBODY... SO PESACH RAN INTO THE DINING ROOM AND YELLED, "INSPECTORS ARE COMING!"

IT WAS NO INSPECTOR, OF COURSE. BUT 40% OF THE GUESTS RAN FAST FROM THE ROOM. ...PESACH HAD ENOUGH DESSERTS LEFT OVER EVEN FOR THE NEXT DAY!

COME.

ARE YOU READY TO WALK AGAIN?

YES, IT'S TOO DIRTY TO SIT! ...BUT, REALLY, IF I DIDN'T HAVE MY NITROSTAT, IT COULD HAVE BEEN JUST NOW SOMETHING TERRIBLE.

MILOCH SPIEGELMAN—HE SURVIVED THE WAR WITH HIS WIFE AND CHILD AND THEY MOVED TO AUSTRALIA. ABOUT FIVE YEARS AGO HE GOT A BIG HEART ATTACK...

AND LAST YEAR, HE GOT ON THE STREET A SEIZURE—LIKE WHAT I HAD JUST NOW... BUT HE DIDN'T HAVE WITH HIM HIS PILLS. HIS WIFE RAN TO FIND A DRUG STORE.

WHEN SHE CAME BACK MILOCH WAS DEAD!

NU? SO LIFE GOES.

BUT I MUST FINISH QUICK TO TELL YOU THE REST ABOUT SRODULA, BECAUSE WE WILL COME SOON OVER TO THE BANK.

SALE

BY THE END OF 1943 THE VANS WENT EVERY WEDNESDAY WITH MORE AND MORE AND MORE PEOPLE FROM SRODULA TO AUSCHWITZ UNTIL IT WAS VERY FEW LEFT.

IT COULD BE OUR TURN SOON, EH VLADEK?

LET'S HOPE NOT, MILOCH.

HASKEL HEARD THAT ANY DAY NOW THEY INTEND TO DEPORT EVERYONE THAT'S STILL LEFT HERE.

MILOCH TOOK ME TO THE SHOE SHOP

IT WAS EARLY AND NOBODY WAS THERE...

HASKEL MADE PLANS TO SMUGGLE HIMSELF OUT OF THE GHETTO.

PESACH AND I HAVE A PLAN ALSO...

HE MOVED A FEW SHOES FROM A PILE HIGH TO THE CEILING...

...AND TOOK ME INSIDE A TUNNEL...

DON'T TELL ANYONE ABOUT THIS EXCEPT ANJA AND YOUR NEPHEW.

...A TUNNEL MADE FROM SHOES!

WE CAME OUT TO A BUNKER...

BE PREPARED TO BRING THEM ON A MOMENT'S NOTICE!

INCREDIBLE!

EVERYTHING WAS READY HERE SO 15 OR 16 PEOPLE COULD HIDE.

...BUT WHEN ANJA AND I APPROACHED TO DISCUSS THIS BUNKER WITH LOLEK...

NO THANKS, FORGET IT!

BUT MILOCH ORGANIZED EVERYTHING!

I'M **SICK** OF HIDING!

OUR NEPHEW WAS THEN ONLY 15. HE WAS WORKING AS AN ELECTRICIAN.

ALWAYS LOLEK WAS A LITTLE MESHUGA...

I'M A SKILLED WORKER. WHEREVER THEY TAKE ME, I'LL BE OKAY.

YOU'RE CRAZY! YOU'RE GOING STRAIGHT TO THE OVENS!

AND HE *DID* GET PUT INTO ONE OF THE NEXT TRANSPORTS TO AUSCHWITZ.

ANJA BECAME COMPLETELY HYSTERICAL.

THE WHOLE FAMILY IS GONE! GRANDMA AND GRANDPA! POPPA! MOMMA! TOSHA! BIBI! MY RICHIEU!!

NOW THEY'LL TAKE LOLEK!

IT WAS ALSO AROUND THIS TIME THAT WE HEARD FIRST THE BAD NEWS FROM ZAWIERCIE-ABOUT TOSHA AND RICHIEU.

OH GOD. LET ME DIE TOO!

COME, ANJA. GET UP!

WHY ARE YOU PULLING ME, VLADEK? LET ME ALONE! I DON'T WANT TO LIVE!

NO, DARLING! TO DIE, IT'S EASY...

BUT YOU HAVE TO STRUGGLE FOR LIFE!

UNTIL THE LAST MOMENT WE MUST STRUGGLE TOGETHER! I NEED YOU!

AND YOU'LL SEE THAT TOGETHER WE'LL SURVIVE.

THIS ALWAY I TOLD TO H

THE GHETTO FINISHED OUT SO LIKE MILOCH SAID. ABOUT TWELVE FROM US RAN INTO HIS BUNKER WITH HIM, HIS WIFE AND HIS THREE-YEARS-OLD BABY BOY.

GUTCHA, YOU'VE GOT TO KEEP THE BABY QUIET!

HUSH.

WAAH! I'M HUNGRY!

WE'LL HAVE TO KEEP HIM UNDER BLANKETS UNTIL HE CALMS DOWN.

IN A BUNKER IN ANOTHER PART FROM THE SHOE SHOP LAY PESACH AND SOME OTHERS.

IT WAS NOTHING TO DO ALL DAY BUT TO LIE AND TO STARVE.

THE WHOLE DAY AND NIGHT ANJA SAT WRITING INTO HER NOTEBOOK.

THERE! I'VE MANAGED TO DIG A SMALL HOLE IN THE STONE WALL.

I CAN SEE SOLDIERS.

ALL AROUND WERE GUARDS TO FIND ANY WHO REMAINED HIDING.

WHAT LITTLE FOOD WE HAD, SOON IT WAS GONE.

OHH...I WISH I HAD SOME BREAD...I WISH I HAD SOME BREAD...I WISH—

QUIET! WE'RE ALL STARVING!

AT NIGHT WE SNEAKED OUT TO LOOK FOR WHAT TO EAT... BUT IT WAS NOTHING TO FIND.

HERE, ANJA— CHEW ON THIS.

YOU FOUND FOOD?

NEVER ANY OF US HAD BEEN SO HUNGRY LIKE THEN.

NO, IT'S ONLY WOOD. BUT CHEWING IT FEELS A LITTLE LIKE EATING FOOD.

AFTER A TIME PESACH CAME OVER TO US FROM HIS BUNKER...

MAYBE YOU FOOLS ARE WILLING TO LIE HERE UNTIL YOU STARVE TO DEATH—BUT NOT ME!...

I'VE CONTACTED ONE OF THE GUARDS.

IT'LL COST A FORTUNE, BUT HE'S AGREED TO LOOK THE OTHER WAY.

OUR GROUP WILL MIX IN WITH THE POLES WHEN THEY WALK PAST SRODULA ON THE WAY TO WORK TOMORROW...
IF YOU WANT TO CHIP IN YOU CAN COME WITH US.

MANY FROM OUR BUNKER SAID YES.

MILOCH AND I, WE SAID NO TO THIS IDEA. WE DIDN'T TRUST TO THE GERMANS.

ONE GUY FROM OUR BUNKER, AVRAM, CAME TO ME.

HE SAID, "TELL ME WHEN **YOU** WILL GO OUT, VLADEK. **THEN** I'LL KNOW IT'S SAFE."

HE AND HIS GIRLFRIEND WANTED TO **PAY** ME TO ADVISE.

THEY HAD STILL 2 WATCHES AND SOME DIAMOND RINGS. I DIDN'T WANT TO TAKE. THEY **NEEDED** THESE TO LIVE.

SO I TOOK ONLY THE SMALL WATCH.

THE NEXT MORNING, VERY EARLY, THE GROUP WALKED OUT.

I STOOD, SECRET, BEHIND A CORNER. I HEARD LOUD SHOOTING, AND I DIDN'T GO TO SEE WHAT HAPPENED...

THEY GAVE OVER THE MONEY AND WENT PAST THE GUARD.

TAKKA TAKKA TAK!

I ONLY RAN VERY FAST BACK TO OUR BUNKER.

ONLY A FEW OF US REMAINED.

THERE HAVEN'T BEEN ANY LIGHTS ON IN THE GUARD-HOUSE FOR TWO NIGHTS... I THINK IT'S SAFE.

A LITTLE BEFORE DAWN WE WENT OUT FROM SRODULA...

THEY'RE ALL GONE!

THE GHETTO IS EMPTY!

WHEW

AHEAD OF TIME WE ORGANIZED OUR-SELVES GOOD CLOTHES AND I.D. PAPERS.

WE MIXED WITH THE POLES GOING TO WORK.

WE'LL BE HIDING AT THIS AD-DRESS. WHEN YOU FIND A SAFE PLACE, TRY TO CONTACT US, VLADEK.

GOOD LUCK, MILOCH.

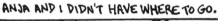

WE WENT ALL IN DIF-FERENT DIRECTIONS.

THAT GUY, AVRAM, HIS WOMAN HAD FRIENDS TO KEEP THEM.

AND THE FRIENDS KEPT THEM... UNTIL AVRAM'S MONEY FINISHED. THEN THEY WERE REPORTED.

ANJA AND I DIDN'T HAVE WHERE TO GO.

WE WALKED IN THE DIRECTION OF SOSNOWIEC - BUT **WHERE TO GO?!**

IT WAS **NOWHERE** WE HAD TO HIDE.

CAN I HELP YOU, MR. SPIEGELMAN?

YES, I HAVE HERE MY SON, ARTIE. I WANT TO SIGN HIM A KEY. SO HE CAN GO ALSO TO MY SAFETY BOX.

IN CASE ANYTHING BAD HAPPENS TO ME YOU MUST RUN *RIGHT AWAY* OVER HERE.

THEREFORE I ARRANGED FOR YOU THIS KEY.

TAKE EVERYTHING OUT FROM THE SAFE. OTHERWISE IT CAN GO ONLY TO TAXES. OR *MALA* WILL GRAB IT.

PLEASE, POP...

TALKING ABOUT YOUR ESTATE JUST MAKES ME UNCOMFORTABLE.

YOU'RE NOW OLD ENOUGH SO WE *MUST* THINK OF THESE THINGS.

WHY DON'T YOU JUST ENJOY YOUR SAVINGS WHILE YOU STILL CAN?

I'LL KEEP IN MY DESK YOUR COPY OF THE KEY. YOU ONLY WOULD LOSE IT!

LOOK, YOU SEE WHAT I HAVE HERE? THIS CIGARETTE CASE AND THE LADY'S POWDER CASE—IT'S 14 KARATS GOLD.

UH HUH

THESE THINGS I HAD WITH ME *THEN*—IN SRODULA, IN THE CHANDELIER BUNKER.

REALLY? HOW CAN YOU POSSIBLY STILL HAVE THEM?

WHEN THE GESTAPO FOUND US I DROPPED *QUICK* A FEW THINGS INTO THE CHIMNEY... IF THEY FOUND THE REST OF MY JEWELS, AT LEAST *THESE* MIGHT REMAIN.

AFTER I CAME OUT FROM THE CAMPS IN 1945 I SNEAKED BACK TO SRODULA AND—AT NIGHT, WHILE THE PEOPLE INSIDE SLEPT—I DIGGED THESE THINGS OUT FROM THE BOTTOM OF THE CHIMNEY.

GOSH.

126

YOU SEE THIS DIAMOND? THIS I GAVE TO ANJA WHEN FIRST WE CAME TO THE U.S.

EVEN WHEN YOU WERE A LITTLE BOY, ANJA WANTED THAT THIS RING SHOULD BE FOR YOUR WIFE.

BUT IF I GIVE IT TO YOU, MALA WILL DRIVE ME CRAZY. SHE WANTS EVERYTHING ONLY FOR HER.

SHE WANTS THAT I GIVE *NOTHING* FOR MY BROTHER IN ISRAEL, AND NOTHING FOR YOU—THREE TIMES ALREADY SHE MADE ME CHANGE OVER MY WILL.

C'MON—MALA'S OKAY!

YOU ONLY CAN'T KNOW! EVEN RIGHT AFTER MY LAST HEART ATTACK, WHEN STILL I WAS IN BED, SHE STARTED *AGAIN* ABOUT CHANGING THE WILL!

I SAID, "MALA, YOU *SEE* HOW SICK I AM. LET ME A LITTLE BIT HAVE SOME PEACE. WHAT YOU *WANT* FROM ME?"

AND SHE SCREAMED, "I WANT THE MONEY! THE MONEY, THE MONEY!"

WHY, ARTIE? WHY I EVER REMARRIED?

OY, ANJA! ANJA! ANJA!

EASY, POP... LET'S GO HOME.

Another visit...

ANYBODY HOME? THE DOOR WASN'T LOCKED, SO I ...

HUH? MALA? WERE YOU CRYING?

NO. SNK I DON'T KNOW. I TELL YOU, I'M AT MY WITS' END!

WHAT NOW?

YOUR FATHER! HE TREATS ME AS IF I WERE JUST A MAID OR HIS NURSE... *WORSE!*

AT LEAST A MAID HAS SOME DAYS OFF AND GETS PAID!

HE ONLY GIVES ME $50.00 A MONTH. WHEN I NEED A PAIR OF STOCKINGS I HAVE TO USE MY OWN SAVINGS!

WELL... HE HASN'T CHANGED...

WHENEVER I NEEDED SCHOOL SUPPLIES OR NEW CLOTHES MOM WOULD HAVE TO PLEAD AND ARGUE FOR *WEEKS* BEFORE HE'D COUGH UP ANY DOUGH!

WHEN *I* TRY TO ARGUE WITH HIM HE MOANS LIKE HE'S GOING TO HAVE ANOTHER HEART ATTACK.

I CAN'T BE SURE IF HE'S FAKING, SO I HAVE TO STOP!

I FEEL LIKE I'M IN PRISON!

I FEEL LIKE I'M GOING TO *BURST!*

COME. WE'LL ALL OF US GO TO THE GARDEN... YOU'LL SEE HOW NICE IT LOOKS, THE BUSHES.

YOU GO! I'VE GOT TO GET READY...

...I HAVE AN APPOINTMENT AT THE HAIRDRESSER'S.

AGAIN TO THE HAIRDRESSER? ONLY A WEEK AGO YOU WENT!

SHE SEES MORE OFTEN THE HAIRDRESSER THAN SHE SEES ME!

WHAT I SAID THAT'S SO TERRIBLE? BELIEVE ME, YOU'D HAVE MORE FRESH AIR FROM THE GARDEN THAN FROM A *HUNDRED* HAIRDRESSERS!

OI, VLADEK. STOP IT!

YOU *SEE* HOW IT IS? ANY TIME I WANT TO GO OUT FOR A FEW MINUTES HE TRIES TO MAKE ME FEEL **GUILTY**!

I'M SUPPOSED TO BE AT HIS CONSTANT BECK AND CALL!

YOU SEE HOW SHE IS? WHAT HAVE I TO DO WITH HER?

C'MON, POP. LET'S GO SIT IN THE GARDEN.

IF I SAY ONLY ONE WORD TO HER, SHE MAKES RIGHT AWAY AN ARGUMENT!

SHE SAYS SHE WANTS TO **LEAVE** ME! I TELL TO HER: "SO? HERE IS THE DOOR. BUT, REMEMBER, IT'S ONLY ONE WAY... IF YOU GO OUT, YOU CAN'T COME BACK!"

MAYBE YOU SHOULD BOTH SEE A MARRIAGE COUNSELOR.

ACH! I DON'T WANT THAT A STRANGER SHOULD MIX INTO OUR PRIVATE STORIES.

TO A **LAWYER** I TALKED, YEARS AGO... AND RIGHT AWAY HE WARNED TO ME: "VLADEK-WATCH OUT. I SEE THAT THIS WOMAN IS MONEY-CONSCIOUS!"

AND ONCE MALA AND I SAT WITH AUNT HELEN TO HELP AGREE US FOR A NEW WILL... BUT A MONTH AFTER, MALA WANTED **AGAIN** TO CHANGE IT.

DON'T SEE A THERAPIST ABOUT YOUR **WILL**... TALK ABOUT HOW TO GET ALONG BETTER.

WITH MALA, IT'S NOT TO GET ALONG. ONLY IT'S THE **MONEY**!

I GIVE UP... I DON'T KNOW WHAT TO SAY.

YOU SEE? I **ALSO** DON'T KNOW WHAT TO SAY!

LOOK. I CAN'T STAY LONG. I NEED TO KNOW MORE ABOUT YOU AND ANJA..

IT'S CHILLY... TAKE ALSO HERE A BLANKET.

NO THANKS. WHAT HAPPENED IN 1944, AFTER YOU LEFT SRODULA?

WE SNEAKED TOWARD SOSNOWIEC...

IT WAS STILL DARK OUTSIDE...WE DIDN'T KNOW WHERE TO HIDE OURSELVES...

JANINA LIVES OVER THERE.

RICHIEU'S GOVERNESS ALWAYS OFFERED SHE WOULD HELP US.

WE CAME TO HER HOUSE NEAR TOWN...

OPEN UP, JANINA! QUICK!

W-WHO'S THERE?

MY GOD! IT'S THE SPIEGELMANS!

YOU'LL BRING TROUBLE! GO AWAY! *QUICKLY!*

SLAM

I'M FRIGHTENED, VLADEK.

MAYBE WE SHOULD TRY MY FATHER'S OLD HOUSE. THE JANITOR HAS KNOWN OUR FAMILY FOR YEARS.

LET'S TRY. WE'VE **GOT** TO GET OFF THE STREETS BEFORE DAWN!

I WAS A LITTLE SAFE. I HAD A COAT AND BOOTS, SO LIKE A GESTAPO WORE WHEN HE WAS NOT IN SERVICE. BUT *ANJA*-HER APPEARANCE-YOU COULD SEE MORE *EASY* SHE WAS JEWISH. I WAS AFRAID FOR HER.

WAKE UP, MR. LUKOWSKI. LET US IN. *PLEASE!!*

HUH? W-WHO IS IT?

ANJA! ANJA ZYLBERBERG!

WHAT ARE YOU DOING HERE, CHILD? IT ISN'T SAF WAIT- I'LL UNLOCK THE GATE.

137

I WALKED SLOW...

BEHIND ME ALSO WALKED SLOW.

CLIK CLIK

IF I WALKED FAST...

BEHIND ME ALSO WALKED FAST.

CLIK

WE WERE ALONE. HE SPOKE...

AMCHA?

IN HEBREW HE SAID TO ME, "OUR NATION?"

HAD I TO ANSWER HIM, OR NO?

A-AMCHA.

I THOUGHT YOU WERE A JEW...

... I'M JEWISH TOO! THERE ARE VERY FEW OF US LEFT...

...MY WIFE AND I HAVE BEEN HIDING IN SOSNOWIEC FOR OVER A YEAR.

I'M WITH MY WIFE TOO. WE'RE HUNGRY AND WE NEED A PLACE TO HIDE!

GO TO THE BLACK MARKET ON DE-KERTA STREET, NUMBER 8.

SO I LEFT HIM AND WENT RIGHT AWAY TO DEKERTA 8. THERE IT WAS A BIG COURTYARD..

?

ALL AROUND I LOOKED, BUT IT WAS NOBODY.

PSSST!

!

WANNA BUY SOME FOOD WITHOUT COUPONS, MISTER?

SHE SHOWED TO ME SAUSAGES, EGGS, CHEESE ...THINGS I ONLY WAS ABLE TO DREAM ABOUT.

I BOUGHT AND WENT QUICK BACK TO ANJA.

GOOD MORNING.

VLADEK! YOU WERE GONE SO LONG.

I HAD TO GET BREAKFAST!... WANT SOME SAUSAGES?...OR EGGS?..OR WOULD YOU PREFER CHOCOLATE?

WHAT?

IT'S A *MIRACLE!* HOW DID YOU MANAGE IT?

I'M A MAGICIAN! HAVE SOME MILK.

I WENT AGAIN BACK TO DEKERTA. THERE I COULD CHANGE JEWELRY FOR MARKS—AND MARKS FOR FOOD, OR A PLACE TO STAY.

THIS TIME IT WAS MORE PEOPLE...THERE EVEN, I SAW SOME JEWISH BOYS I KNEW FROM BEFORE THE WAR.

VLADEK SPIEGELMAN?! I HARDLY RECOGNIZED YOU. SO YOU'RE STILL ALIVE, EH?

LEO? YES. I'M WITH ANJA.

WE NEED A HIDING PLACE.

HOW ABOUT MRS. KAWKA?

SHE HAS A SMALL FARM ON THE OUTSKIRTS OF TOWN...

SHE MIGHT TAKE YOU IN, IF YOU CAN PAY.

IT WAS NOT SO FAR TO GO TO KAWKA'S FARM...

ALRIGHT THEN, MR. SPIEGELMAN. YOU AND YOUR WIFE CAN STAY IN MY BARN.

WE'LL COME LATE TONIGHT.

BUT, REMEMBER-IF YOU'RE FOUND THERE, I DON'T KNOW YOU! ... YOU MUST SAY THAT THE BARN DOOR WAS OPEN AND YOU JUST SNEAKED IN.

DON'T WORRY...WE WON'T BETRAY YOU!

IT'S ALMOST DAWN—WHEN MRS. KAWKA COMES TO MILK HER COW, SHE'LL BRING YOU SOME COFFEE.

WHERE ARE YOU GOING?

TO DEKERTA.

AND SO WE CAME THERE TO LIVE WITH KAWKA'S COW.

DON'T LEAVE ME ALONE AGAIN. I'M **TERRIFIED** WHILE YOU'RE GONE.

DON'T WORRY, ANJA. I'LL BE SAFE. IF I DIDN'T GO OUT WE WOULDN'T HAVE **FOOD**...WE WOULDN'T HAVE *THIS* PLACE!...

AND WE'VE **GOT** TO FIND A WARMER PLACE FOR THE WINTER...AWAY FROM SOSNOWIEC IF POSSIBLE...

I—I'LL BE OKAY. COME BACK QUICK.

I TRAVELED OFTEN WITH THE STREETCAR TO TOWN.

IT WAS TWO CARS. ONE WAS ONLY GERMANS AND OFFICIALS. THE SECOND, IT WAS ONLY THE POLES.

ALWAYS I WENT STRAIGHT IN THE **OFFICIAL** CAR...

HEIL HITLER.

THE GERMANS PAID NO ATTENTION OF ME.... IN THE PO-LISH CAR THEY COULD **SMELL** IF A POLISH JEW CAME IN.

140

AT THE BLACK MARKET I SAW SEVERAL TIMES A NICE WOMAN, WHAT I MADE A LITTLE FRIENDS WITH HER...

GOOD MORNING, MR. SPIEGELMAN.

HOW DO YOU DO, MRS. MOTONOWA! WHAT DO YOU HAVE IN YOUR BASKET TODAY?

HOW ABOUT A LOAF OF FRESH BREAD?

FINE, FINE.

OH. I'M SORRY. I DON'T HAVE ANY CHANGE.

IT'S OKAY... KEEP IT FOR YOUR LITTLE BOY.

ARE YOU AND YOUR WIFE STILL LIVING IN A BARN?

WE HAVEN'T FOUND ANYTHING BETTER.

I'VE BEEN THINKING ABOUT IT... WHY DON'T YOU BOTH MOVE IN WITH MY SON AND ME?

WHAT ABOUT YOUR HUSBAND?

HE WORKS IN GERMANY, AND ONLY COMES HOME FOR 10 DAYS EVERY 3 MONTHS ... I'LL KEEP YOU HIDDEN IN THE CELLAR WHEN HE'S AROUND.

IT SOUNDS GOOD TO ME, BUT IT'S OVER 20 KILOMETERS TO YOUR HOUSE IN SZOPIENICE. MY WIFE WILL BE AFRAID TO GO!

DON'T WORRY. I'LL ESCORT YOU!

THE NEXT EVENING SHE CAME WITH HER 7-YEARS-OLD BOY TO KAWKA'S FARMHOUSE...

I WALKED WITH MOTONOWA AS IF *SHE* WAS MY WIFE.

AND ANJA, LIKE A GOVERNESS, WENT WITH THE LITTLE BOY BEHIND. AND NOBODY EVEN *LOOKED* ON US.

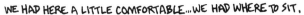
WE HAD HERE A LITTLE COMFORTABLE...WE HAD WHERE TO SIT,

REMEMBER, LITTLE ONE—NEVER TELL **ANYBODY** THERE ARE JEWS HERE. THEY'LL **SHOOT US ALL!**

YES, AUNT ANJA.

THE LITTLE BOY WAS VERY SMART AND HE LOVED VERY MUCH ANJA.

YOU HAD TO **PAY** MRS. MOTONOWA TO KEEP YOU, RIGHT?

OF COURSE I PAID... AND **WELL** I PAID.

...WHAT YOU THINK? SOMEONE WILL RISK THEIR LIFE FOR NOTHING?

...I PAID ALSO FOR THE **FOOD** WHAT SHE GAVE TO US FROM HER SMUGGLING BUSINESS.

BUT, ONE TIME I MISSED A FEW COINS TO THE BREAD...

I'LL PAY YOU THE REST TOMORROW, AFTER I GO OUT AND CASH SOME VALUABLES.

SORRY... I WASN'T ABLE TO **FIND** ANY BREAD TODAY.

ALWAYS SHE GOT BREAD, SO I DIDN'T BELIEVE... BUT, STILL, SHE WAS A GOOD WOMAN.

IN HIS SCHOOL THE BOY WAS VERY BAD IN GERMAN. SO ANJA TUTORED TO HIM.

ICH BIN... DU BIST.. ER IST...

SHE KNEW GERMAN LIKE AN EXPERT.

AND SOON HE CAME OUT WITH **VERY** GOOD GRADES,

MY TEACHER ASKED ME HOW I IMPROVED SO MUCH...

SO I TOLD HIM MY **MOTHER** WAS HELPING ME.

WHEW

HE WAS REALLY A CLEVER BOY.

BUT IT WAS A FEW THINGS HERE NOT SO GOOD... HER HOME WAS VERY SMALL AND IT WAS ON THE GROUND FLOOR...

BE SURE TO KEEP AWAY FROM THE WINDOW — YOU MIGHT BE SEEN!

NOK NOK

ONE MINUTE!

(QUICK – GET IN THE CLOSET!)

IF SOMEBODY CAME, WE HAD FAST TO HIDE.

A LETTER FROM YOUR HUSBAND, MRS. MOTONOWA.

THANKS.

BUT I HAD SOMETHING ALLERGIC IN THE CLOSET.

AAH.

OR MAYBE IT WAS A COLD – I CAN'T REMEMBER...

– CHMF

BUT ALWAYS I HAD TO SNEEZE.

STILL, EVERYTHING HERE WAS FINE, UNTIL ONE SATURDAY MOTONOWA RAN VERY EARLY BACK FROM HER BLACK MARKET WORK...

THIS IS TERRIBLE!

THE GESTAPO JUST SEARCHED ME – THEY TOOK MY GOODS!

THEY MAY COME SEARCH HERE ANY MINUTE! YOU'VE GOT TO LEAVE!

WHAT?

BUT WHERE CAN WE GO?

I DON'T KNOW. BUT YOU MUST GET OUT NOW!

OH MY GOD... THIS IS THE END!

ANJA STARTED TO CRY... BUT WE HAD NOT A CHOICE.

WE'LL WALK TOWARD SOS-NOWIEC - AT LEAST WE'LL KNOW OUR WAY AROUND.

ANJA WAS SO AFRAID SHE WAS SHAKING.

STAY CALM - WALK AS IF WE'RE JUST STROLLING... AND *SPEAK GERMAN*.

FOR HOURS WE WALKED.

B-BESUCHEN WIR DOCH FRAU KAWKA.

GUTE IDEE.

VLADEK-WE'RE BEING FOLLOWED.

RELAX

BUT IF WE TURNED A COR-NER, THEY ALSO TURNED.

ES IST KALT.

JA. JA.

OF COURSE I WAS RIGHT - THEY DIDN'T MEAN *ANYTHING* ON US.

WOOSH

THEY JUST WERE WALKING.

STAYING ON THE STREET ALL NIGHT IS TOO DANGEROUS.... MAYBE WE CAN HIDE IN THAT CONSTRUCTION SITE.

GOOD-I'M EXHAUSTED.

HERE WAS A FOUNDATION MADE VERY DEEP DOWN IN THE GROUND..

BE CAREFUL!

I JUMPED FIRST IN, AND I PULLED OVER BRICKS FOR ANJA TO STEP DOWN.

AND HERE WE WAITED A COLD FEW HOURS FOR THE DAY.

144

IT STARTED TO BE LIGHT...

COME. WE WON'T BE NOTICED IF WE MIX WITH PEOPLE OUT ON THE STREET.

I'M SO TIRED AND COLD...

WE CAN REST NOW.

WE CAME FINALLY AGAIN TO THIS PLACE WITH THE COW AND WENT INSIDE.

LATER, KAWKA CAME IN...

W-WHO'S IN HERE?

THE SPIEGEL-MANS... WE HAD NOWHERE ELSE TO GO.

WELL... I GUESS YOU CAN STAY. BUT, REMEMBER: I DON'T KNOW YOU'RE HERE!

WHY, MRS. SPIEGELMAN, YOU'RE SHIVERING!

YOU CAN COME INTO MY HOUSE FOR AN HOUR OR SO, 'TIL YOU WARM UP.

SHE TOOK ANJA INSIDE AND BROUGHT TO ME SOME FOOD...IN THOSE DAYS I WAS SO STRONG I COULD SIT EVEN IN THE SNOW ALL NIGHT...

THINGS CAN'T BE THIS BAD EVERYWHERE! I'D GIVE ANYTHING TO GET OUT OF POLAND!

YOU KNOW, BEFORE I TOOK YOU IN, I HAD A YOUNG MAN AND HIS SON HERE...

TWO PEOPLE I KNOW SMUG-GLED THEM INTO HUNGARY. I HEARD HE AND HIS BOY WERE DOING WELL THERE.

HUNGARY! REALLY?! I'D LIKE TO MEET THOSE SMUGGLERS!

SHE TOLD ME THESE TWO ACQUAINTANCES VISITED OFTEN TO HER ON THURSDAY EVENINGS... TODAY WAS MAYBE A MONDAY...

I DON'T GET IT... WASN'T HUNGARY AS DANGEROUS AS POLAND?

NO. FOR A LONGER TIME IT WAS *BETTER* THERE IN HUNGARY FOR THE JEWS... BUT THEN, NEAR THE VERY FINISH OF THE WAR, THEY ALL GOT PUT *ALSO* TO AUSCHWITZ.

I WAS THERE, AND I SAW IT. THOUSANDS— HUNDREDS OF THOUSANDS OF JEWS FROM HUNGARY...

SO MANY, IT WASN'T EVEN ROOM ENOUGH TO BURY THEM ALL IN THE OVENS.

BUT AT THAT TIME, WHEN I WAS THERE WITH KAWKA, WE COULDN'T *KNOW* THEN.

SO... I WENT NEXT DAY TO DEKERTA STREET TO BUY FOOD...

OH GOD! OH GOD! MR. SPIEGELMAN. YOU'RE ALIVE! I'M SO GLAD TO SEE YOU!

MRS. MOTONOWA!

I WANTED TO FIND A NEW CONNECTION TO HIDE US. BUT *REALLY* I DIDN'T THINK TO FIND AGAIN *HER*.

PRAISE MARY. YOU'RE SAFE! I COULDN'T *SLEEP*, I FELT SO GUILTY ABOUT CHASING YOU AND YOUR WIFE OUT.

THE GESTAPO NEVER EVEN CAME TO MY HOUSE. I JUST PANICKED FOR NOTHING.

PLEASE COME BACK AGAIN.

ANJA WAS GLAD OF GOING BACK. AND MOTONOWA ALSO... ALWAYS I PAID HER NICELY.

AND THAT SAME NIGHT WE SAID GOODBYE TO KAWKA AND WENT AGAIN TO SZOPIENICE.

AFTER WE WERE BACK ONLY A SHORT TIME...

WELL, MY HUSBAND WRITES THAT HE'S COMING HOME FOR HIS 10-DAY VACATION,

IF HE KNEW YOU WERE HERE HE'D THROW US **ALL** OUT. BUT, DON'T WORRY... YOU'LL BE ALL RIGHT IN MY CELLAR.

...I SET UP A MATTRESS... I'LL COME DOWN WHEN-EVER I CAN.

SO EACH DAY AND NIGHT WE SAT IN SUCH A STORAGE LOCKER...

IN THE DAYS WE WERE AFRAID TO BREATHE—PEOPLE CAME DOWN OFTEN TO **THEIR** LOCKERS.

AT NIGHT WE COULD MOVE AROUND A LITTLE, BUT IT WAS SOMETHING ELSE DOWN THERE...

AIEEE!

WH-WHAT IS IT?

TH-THERE ARE **RATS** DOWN HERE!

SHH- CALM DOWN, STOP SCREAMING.

THOSE AREN'T RATS. THEY'RE VERY SMALL. ONE RAN OVER MY HAND BEFORE. THEY'RE JUST **MICE!**

OF COURSE, IT **WAS** REALLY RATS. BUT I WANTED ANJA TO FEEL MORE EASY.

BUT, THEN, MOTONOWA STOPPED TO COME DOWN.

IT'S BEEN 3 DAYS SINCE SHE BROUGHT ANY FOOD.

HERE...HAVE ANOTHER CANDY...

I HAD STILL CANDIES I ORGANIZED ON DEKERTA. ONLY **THIS** WE HAD TO EAT.

ALSO, HERE WE HAD NO PLACE WHERE TO WASH, SO ANJA GOT ON ALL HER SKIN A TERRIBLE RASH.

I DON'T KNOW WHAT'S WORSE—THE HUNGER OR THE ITCHING.

DON'T SCRATCH! IT ONLY—SHH!

CLIK

THE DOOR.

I'M SORRY I COULDN'T GET DOWN BEFORE...MY HUSBAND IS GETTING SUSPICIOUS.

HE ASKED WHY I GO TO THE CELLAR SO OFTEN. HE EVEN ASKED IF I WAS HIDING JEWS HERE! ...HE WAS JOKING, BUT STILL...

ARE YOU ALL RIGHT HERE?

THERE ARE **RATS**, GIANT RATS! THEY'RE HORRIBLE!

WELL—YOU'RE BETTER OFF WITH THE RATS THAN WITH THE GESTAPO... AT LEAST THE RATS WON'T **KILL** YOU!

MMM..

AND SHE WAS RIGHT. WE WERE HAPPY EVEN TO HAVE **THESE** CONDITIONS.

AFTER THE TEN DAYS HER HUSBAND LEFT, AND SHE TOOK US BACK.

IT'S GOOD TO BE "HOME," EH, VLADEK?

IT'S A LOT NICER THAN THAT CELLAR.

BUT I DIDN'T FEEL SAFE HERE. IT WAS TOO MANY WAYS SOMEBODY COULD FIND US OUT. I WANTED TO GO BETTER TO HUNGARY.

SO, WHEN IT CAME THURSDAY, I WENT IN THE DIRECTION TO TAKE A STREETCAR TO SEE KAWKA IN SOSNOWIEC.

LOOK!

I HAD TO PASS WHERE SOME CHILDREN WERE PLAYING.

A JEW! A JEW!

THEY RAN SCREAMING HOME.

HELP! MOMMY! A JEW!!

A JEW!

QUICK, THE MOTHERS CAME OUTSIDE TO SEE WHAT WAS!

THE MOTHERS ALWAYS TOLD SO: "BE CAREFUL! A JEW WILL CATCH YOU TO A BAG AND EAT YOU!" ... SO THEY TAUGHT TO THEIR CHILDREN.

I APPROACHED OVER TO THEM...

HEIL HITLER.

IF I RAN AWAY THEY, WOULD SEE: "YES, IT IS A JEW HERE."

DON'T BE AFRAID, LITTLE ONES. I'M NOT A JEW. I WON'T HURT YOU.

SORRY, MISTER. YOU KNOW HOW KIDS ARE ... HEIL HITLER.

SO I CAME OUT WELL FROM THIS...

BUT THE EXPERIENCE COST ME REALLY A LOT OF HAIRS.

WHEN I ARRIVED TO KAWKA, THE TWO SMUGGLERS WERE THERE TOGETHER SITTING IN THE KITCHEN..

PLEASE WAIT IN THE OTHER ROOM. THEY'LL SEE YOU SOON.

MR. MANDELBAUM!

VLADEK SPIEGELMAN!

MANDELBAUM, BEFORE THE WAR OWNED A SWEETS SHOP.

ANJA AND I BOUGHT ALWAYS PASTRIES THERE. HE USED TO BE A VERY RICH MAN IN SOSNOWIEC.

THIS IS MY WIFE...AND YOU KNOW MY NEPHEW..

HELLO, ABRAHAM. WHAT ARE YOU ALL DOING HERE?

BACK WHEN IT WAS THE GHETTO, ABRAHAM WAS A BIG MEMBER OF THE JEWISH COUNCIL

WE'RE TRYING TO GET OUT OF POLAND—

—TO HUNGARY?! YES. ANJA AND I ARE TRYING TO ARRANGE THAT TOO!

THE SMUGGLERS PROPOSED US HOW THEY WOULD DO.

...AND AT THE BORDER OUR PARTNERS WILL TAKE YOU THROUGH THE MOUNTAINS.

WHEW— IT'S RISKY AND VERY EXPENSIVE!

WE SPOKE YIDDISH SO THE POLES DON'T UNDERSTAND.

NIE, VAS DENKST DIE?

YECH KENN DIE FRAU KAWKA, UBER YECH BIN NISH ZICHER VEGEN DIE ZWEI.

So, what do you think?

I know Mrs. Kawka, but I'm not sure about these two.

HERR MECHTSE! YECH GEI KOIDEM MIT ZEI. AZ ALLES VET ZEIN BESEDER, YECH VIL SCHREIBEN TSE DEYER.

Listen! I'll go first. If everything is okay, I'll write back to you.

THE OTHERS WANT TO THINK ABOUT IT A LITTLE LONGER, BUT I'M READY TO GO NOW.

FINE, FINE.

I AGREED WITH MANDELBAUM TO MEET AGAIN HERE. IF IT CAME A GOOD LETTER, WE'LL GO.

BUT IF EVER I TALKED OF THIS PLAN TO ANJA...

NO, VLADEK! YOU'RE CRAZY! IT'S TOO DANGEROUS!

BUT IF WE HEAR FROM ABRAHAM—

WE'RE SAFE HERE- FORGET ABOUT HUNGARY!

BUT WHAT DO WE DO IF THE GESTAPO COMES TO SEARCH FOR ILLEGAL GOODS? ...WHAT IF A NEIGHBOR NOTICES US THROUGH THE KITCHEN WINDOW?...

I'M NOT GOING!

WHAT IF HER HUSBAND FINDS OUT ABOUT US? EVEN THE BOY COULD LET SOMETHING SLIP! ...THIS WAR COULD LAST ANOTHER 4 OR 5 YEARS. WHAT DO WE DO WHEN OUR MONEY RUNS OUT?

PLEASE!

IN HUNGARY WE COULD BE FREE TO WALK THE STREETS AGAIN, LIKE HUMAN BEINGS... I'VE ALWAYS TAKEN CARE OF YOU- TRUST ME.

I'M SO SCARED. ≥SOB≤

DON'T DO IT, MR. SPIEGELMAN— IT'S JUST NOT SAFE! YOU DON'T KNOW ANYTHING ABOUT THESE SMUGGLERS.

SNF. IT'S LIKE TALKING TO A WALL.

WE WON'T GO UNLESS WE HEAR THAT OUR FRIEND GOT THROUGH.

I'VE HAD AWFUL NIGHTMARES ABOUT YOUR TRIP- PLEASE STAY WITH ME!

SNF

WAIT- NOW WHERE ARE YOU GOING?

-TO VISIT MY COUSIN AND SEE WHERE HE'S HIDING. IF WE DO GO TO HUNGARY, HE MAY BE BETTER OFF HERE WITH YOU!

MILOCH HELPED ME IN SRODULA. MAYBE NOW, IF HE NEEDED, I COULD HELP HIM.

THE JANITOR IN THE HOUSE MILOCH OWNED, SHE HID NOW HIM AND HIS FAMILY; BUT —OH BOY— HE WAS IN A SITUATION WORSE AS I COULD IMAGINE!

I WENT TO THE JANITOR BY TROLLEY

HELLO— I'M MILOCH'S COUSIN, VLADEK.

YES. HE TOLD ME YOU MIGHT COME.

I HAVE SOME COMPANY UPSTAIRS. I CAN'T TAKE YOU TO MILOCH UNTIL THEY LEAVE.

GENTLEMEN. THIS IS MY COUSIN, VLADEK.

HI "CUZ," HAVE A DRINK.

SO WE TALKED, AND THEY BELIEVED I AM *HER* COUSIN.

WE'RE ALMOST OUT OF VODKA. BRING SOME MORE, MEINKA.

THERE ISN'T ANY.

BAH! SHE'S **HIDING** HER VODKA!

JUST LIKE SHE'S HIDING JEWS IN HER YARD!

THE JANITOR AND I FROZE OUR BLOOD FROM FEAR...

IF YOU DON'T PUT ANOTHER BOTTLE ON THE TABLE *RIGHT AWAY*, WE'LL TELL THE GESTAPO ABOUT THE JEWS YOU'RE KEEPING!!

R-RELAX FELLOWS

HERE'S A FEW MARKS, MEINKA. RUN DOWNSTAIRS AND GET ANOTHER BOTTLE FOR OUR FRIENDS.

'ATTA BOY. HIC.

IN 15 MINUTES SHE CAME WITH A BOTTLE AND THEY WERE HAPPY.

YOU SEE? YOUR COUSIN KNOWS HOW TO ENTERTAIN GUESTS! TO YOUR HEALTH.

WE DRANK AND WE DRANK— ONLY NEAR MIDNIGHT FINALLY THEY WENT HOME.

I THINK IT'S SAFE TO GO DOWN.

ARE YOU -SNF- CARRYING FOOD FOR MILOCH?

I FED THEM EARLIER. THIS IS JUST TRASH.

THE CONDITIONS HOW MILOCH WAS LIVING-YOU COULDN'T BELIEVE.

...I ALWAYS BRING GARBAGE SO THE NEIGHBORS DON'T GET SUSPICIOUS.

PSST-MILOCH. YOUR COUSIN IS HERE.

?

IN EACH COURTYARD WAS A VERY DEEP HOLE TO THROW IN ALL THE GARBAGE.

INSIDE THIS GARBAGE HOLE WAS HERE SEPARATED A TINY SPACE — MAYBE ONLY 5 FEET BY 6 FEET.

VLADEK! I'M GLAD YOU'RE STILL ALIVE!

MY GOD!

I LOOKED DOWN ONLY FOR A SECOND, BUT IN THERE WAS LIVING MILOCH, HIS WIFE AND THEIR 3-YEARS-OLD BOY.

HOW CAN YOU LIVE THERE? YOU MUST BE FREEZING!

WE HAVE NO CHOICE. AT LEAST OUR BUNKKER IS UNDERGROUND..

AND THE DECOMPOSING GARBAGE GIVES SOME HEAT.

BUT PEOPLE KNOW YOU'RE IN THERE...

I TOLD HIM MY STORY WITH THESE POLES UPSTAIRS.

WHAT CAN WE DO?

LISTEN- ANJA AND I MAY BE GOING TO HUNGARY!..

I EXPLAINED OUR HIDING PLACE WAS NOT PERFECT, BUT BETTER THAN HIS.

I'LL COME AGAIN WHEN I HAVE MORE NEWS, BUT IT'S VERY LATE NOW— I MUST GET BACK HOME.

AND I WAS LUCKY. NOBODY MADE ME ANY QUESTIONS GOING BACK TO SZOPIENICE.

A FEW DAYS AFTER, I CAME AGAIN TO THE SMUGGLERS. AND MANDELBAUM WAS ALSO THERE.

LOOK, VLADEK— MY NEPHEW IS SAFE! THEY BROUGHT ME A LETTER FROM HIM.

IT WAS IN YIDDISH AND IT WAS SIGNED REALLY BY ABRAHAM, SO WE AGREED RIGHT AWAY TO GO AHEAD.

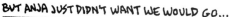

BUT ANJA JUST DIDN'T WANT WE WOULD GO...

PLEASE, VLADEK, CALL IT OFF!

BUT IT'S ALL AR- RANGED. I'VE EVEN GIVEN THEM HALF THEIR MONEY!

NO! NO! NO! IT'S SOME KIND OF TRICK!

BE REASONABLE. I SAW ABRAHAM'S LETTER WITH MY OWN EYES!

WH-WHAT DID IT SAY?

"DEAR AUNT AND UNCLE, EVERYTHING IS WON- DERFUL HERE. I AR- RIVED SAFELY. I'M FREE AND HAPPY. DON'T LOSE A MINUTE. JOIN ME AS SOON AS YOU CAN. YOUR LOVING NEPHEW, ABRAHAM."

I-I DON'T KNOW...

WE LEAVE THE DAY AFTER TOMORROW FROM THE KA- TOWICE TRAIN STATION.

AND FINALLY I CONVINCED HER.

SO, I WENT ONE MORE TIME OVER TO MILOCH IN HIS GAR- BAGE BUNKER AND DIRECTED HIM HOW HE MUST GO TO SZOPIENICE AND HIDE...

AND, YOU KNOW, MILOCH AND HIS WIFE AND BOY, THEY ALL SURVIVED THEMSELVES THE WHOLE WAR... SITTING THERE ... WITH MOTONOWA...

BUT, FOR ANJA AND I, IT WAS FOR US WAITING ANOTHER DESTINY...

WE CAME WITH NO PROBLEM BY TROLLEY CAR TO OUR MEET- ING POINT WITH THE MANDEL- BAUMS AND THE SMUGGLERS.

EVERYTHING IS ARRANGED. HERE ARE YOUR TICKETS.

I HAD A SMALL BAG TO TRAVEL. WHEN THEY REGISTERED ME IN, THEY LOOKED OVER EVERYTHING.

WHAT'S THIS? SHOE POLISH??

YES. I LIKE TO KEEP MYSELF NEAT.

WITH A SPOON HE TOOK OUT, LITTLE BY LITTLE, ALL THE POLISH.

WELL, WELL...A GOLD WATCH. YOU JEWS *ALWAYS* HAVE GOLD!

WRAPPED IN FOIL, I KEPT IT HIDDEN THERE... IT WAS MY LAST TREASURE.

IT WAS THIS WATCH I GOT FROM FATHER-IN-LAW WHEN FIRST I MARRIED TO ANJA.

WELL, NEVER MIND...THEY TOOK IT AND THREW ME WITH MANDELBAUM INTO A CELL...

WAIT A MINUTE! WHAT EVER HAPPENED TO ABRAHAM?

WHO?

AH, MANDELBAUM'S NEPHEW! YES. HE FINISHED THE SAME AS US TO CONCENTRATION CAMP.

YES. I'LL TELL YOU HOW IT WAS WITH HIM - BUT NOW I'M TELLING HERE IN THE PRISON...

-BUT

HERE WE GOT VERY LITTLE TO EAT—MAYBE SOUP ONE TIME A DAY—AND WE SAT WITH NOTHING TO DO.

WHY DON'T THEY PUT US TO WORK LIKE THE REST OF YOU?

IT MEANS YOU WON'T BE HERE VERY LONG...

...EVERY WEEK OR SO A TRUCK TAKES SOME OF THE PRISONERS AWAY.

EXCUSE ME.... DO ANY OF YOU KNOW GERMAN?

MY FAMILY JUST SENT ME A FOOD PARCEL. IF I WRITE BACK THEY'LL SEND ANOTHER, BUT WE'RE ONLY ALLOWED TO WRITE GERMAN.

I KNEW **WELL** TO WRITE GERMAN...SO I WROTE....

IN A SHORT TIME HE GOT AGAIN A PACKAGE...

YOU DID A GREAT JOB! TAKE ANYTHING YOU WANT FOR YOU AND YOUR FRIEND!

IT WAS EGGS THERE...IT WAS EVEN CHOCOLATES ...I WAS VERY LUCKY TO GET SUCH GOODIES!

MY GOD.

YES. SO IT WAS...

...AND WHEN THEY OPENED THE TRUCK, THEY PUSHED MEN ONE WAY, WOMEN TO THE OTHER WAY...

ANJA AND I WENT EACH IN A DIFFERENT DIRECTION, AND WE COULDN'T KNOW IF EVER WE'LL SEE EACH OTHER ALIVE AGAIN.

THIS IS WHERE MOM'S DIARIES WILL BE **ESPECIALLY** USEFUL. THEY'LL GIVE ME SOME IDEA OF WHAT SHE WENT THROUGH WHILE YOU WERE APART.

I CAN TELL YOU ... SHE WENT THROUGH THE SAME WHAT ME: TERRIBLE!

IT'S GETTING COLD. WHY DON'T WE GO UPSTAIRS AND SEE IF WE CAN FIND HER NOTEBOOKS...

NO... I **LOOKED** ALREADY...

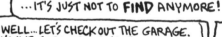

...IT'S JUST NOT TO **FIND** ANYMORE!

WELL... LET'S CHECK OUT THE GARAGE. YOU'VE GOT LOADS OF STUFF IN THERE.

NO. YOU'LL NOT FIND IT. BECAUSE I **REMIND** TO MYSELF WHAT HAPPENED...

THESE NOTEBOOKS, AND OTHER REALLY NICE THINGS OF MOTHER... ONE TIME I HAD A VERY BAD DAY... AND ALL OF THESE THINGS I **DESTROYED.**

YOU **WHAT?**

art spiegelman